I0459105

WIRED

TO

WIN

*A Masterclass in Winning
Strategies from Top Experts*

COMPILED AND EDITED BY
SUZANNE EVANS AND **MARION JONES**
WITH AN INTRODUCTION BY
SUZANNE EVANS

Published by
Driven International, Inc.
50101 Governors Drive
Suite 150
Chapel Hill, NC 27517

Copyright © 2025 by Suzanne Evans and Marion Jones

All rights reserved. No part of this book may be reproduced or transmitted in any form or by any means, electronic or mechanical, including photocopying, recording, or by any information storage and retrieval system, without the written permission of the Publisher, except where permitted by law.

Manufactured in the United States of America, or in the United Kingdom when distributed elsewhere.

Evans, Suzanne and Jones, Marion
Wired To Win
   ISBN: 978-1-953586-35-3
   eBook: 978-1-953586-34-6

Cover design by: Bixby Elliot
Copyediting by: Wendie Pecharsky
Interior design by: Amit Dey
Author photos by: Nikki Incandela and Leslie Bohm

Limit of Liability/Disclaimer of Warranty: While the authors have used their best efforts in preparing this book, they make no representations or warranties with the respect to the accuracy or completeness of the contents of this book and specifically disclaim any implied warranties of merchantability or fitness for a particular purpose. No warranty may be created or extended by sales representatives or sales materials. The advice and strategies contained herein may not be suitable for your situation. You should consult with a professional where appropriate. The authors shall not be liable for damages arising here from.

https://DrivenInc.com

TABLE OF CONTENTS

Table of Contents

INTRODUCTION

Suzanne Evans

Let me make one thing clear before we go any further: You don't have to be perfect to win.

You just have to be **willing**.

Willing to get knocked down, willing to look foolish, willing to keep going when everything in your life—your bank account, your childhood trauma, your calendar full of broken promises—is telling you to sit down and shut up.

That's what it means to be **Wired to Win**.

It's not about some lightning bolt moment of greatness. It's not a gift from God bestowed on the lucky or the tall or the photogenic. It's not a TED Talk, a morning routine or an algorithm you can crack if you just try hard enough.

It's a decision.

And I've made that decision more times than I can count—usually while sitting on the floor, surrounded by unpaid bills, dirty laundry, and gigantic dreams.

I have always had grit, big dreams, and a mother who believed that working hard meant something—even if the world told you otherwise. I worked as an administrative assistant to a Broadway producer, earning $40,000 a year. I started my own business and built it into a multimillion-dollar company helping other people rise.

Why? Because I refused to believe my wiring was broken. I refused to believe that the mess of my past meant I didn't deserve a powerful future.

And neither do you.

Winning Isn't a Trophy. It's a Trait.

Some people hear the word *win* and immediately think about gold medals, big stages, flashy cars, and first-place ribbons.

But if you're here—reading this book—then you know better.

You know that *winning* looks a lot messier than that. Winning is walking into a job interview after being laid off for the third time. Winning is putting down the bottle. Winning is choosing therapy instead of another toxic relationship. Winning is getting up when it's easier to disappear.

The people you'll read about in this book? They're not superhuman. They're not selling you perfection.

They're showing you their scar tissue.

They're letting you peek behind the curtain of their highlight reel to show you what winning really takes: consistency, courage, and a willingness to be wrong again and again, until you get it right.

Because here's the truth: The most successful people you know aren't the smartest. They're not the most educated. They're not the ones with the perfect morning routine and a Pinterest-worthy vision board.

They're the ones who show up, even when it's hard.

Especially when it's hard.

My Wiring Wasn't Natural—It Was Built

There's a chapter in my life that I don't talk about often, but I will now.

It's the part where I had no clue what I was doing. (Spoiler alert: That's most of it.)

I didn't have a business degree. I didn't have a coach. I didn't have a blueprint, but I had a gut feeling and a need. I needed to make money. I needed to prove something to myself. I needed to claw my way out of a life that felt like settling—and I needed to do it fast.

So, I said yes before I was ready. I offered help I wasn't sure I could give. I stumbled, I cried, I apologized, I burned bridges, I built new ones.

And somewhere in the rubble of all that chaos, I realized something:

I was winning.

Not because it was easy, but because I kept showing up, because I kept taking the next step, even when the path looked like a damn cliff.

That's what this book is about.

The people who are *Wired to Win* aren't fearless. They're not delusional. They're not pretending everything's fine when it's not.

They're just people who've learned how to keep moving forward—even when the world is crumbling.

What It Really Means to Be Wired to Win

Let me give it to you straight.

To be Wired to Win means:

- You do it scared.
- You do it tired.
- You do it anyway.
- You stop waiting for permission.
- You stop explaining your dreams to people committed to misunderstanding you.
- You stop outsourcing your power to people who wouldn't last a day in your shoes.

When you're Wired to Win, you realize:

- Obstacles are invitations.
- Setbacks are setups.
- Fear is a compass.

You stop mistaking perfection for power. You stop looking at failure as a life sentence. You stop waiting for the "right moment" and realize that the right moment is usually the one you make.

You start to understand that resilience isn't a bonus trait—it's the foundation. It's not about bouncing back to the person you were before the setback. It's about bouncing forward into someone stronger, wiser, and more aligned with your purpose.

You learn how to alchemize pain into purpose, fear into fuel, and doubt into a doorway. That's the transformation. That's the shift. That's the difference between people who wait for luck—and people who build their lives brick by gritty brick.

You become the kind of person who turns rejection letters into fuel, who sees obstacles as puzzle pieces, and who uses failure as a mirror—not a verdict.

You find the courage to stand in a room full of experts and say, "I belong here." You raise your hand even when your voice shakes. You own your worth like it's your birthright—because it is.

You learn to love the part of yourself that refuses to die, the part that still whispers, "Try again," when everything in you wants to quit.

That's not delusion. That's drive.

Every author in this book has a different story, but they all have one thing in common:

They kept going.

They refused to believe their lowest moment was their final chapter.

And that's what makes them winners.

Let's Redefine Winning

Let's be honest. The world has sold us some garbage definitions of what it means to win:

- More money.
- More likes.
- More followers.
- More hustle.

Let me offer an alternative.

Winning means:

- You speak up when you used to stay quiet.
- You rest without guilt.
- You forgive without forgetting.
- You choose progress over perfection.
- You show up in rooms you used to avoid.
- You say no without apologizing.
- You say yes to yourself.

Winning means:

- You are proud of who you're becoming.
- You walk into your day knowing that your value isn't up for negotiation.
- You make peace with your past and partner with your potential.
- You stop comparing your journey to someone else's highlight reel.
- You measure success in peace of mind, not approval ratings.

It means you no longer define yourself by your worst day. It means you no longer need applause to validate your voice. It means you've stopped keeping score with people who were never playing the same game as you.

It's letting go of needing to be the best and choosing to be your best. It's looking at your reflection and seeing strength where you used to see shame. It's knowing that your joy is your rebellion, your boundaries are your brilliance, your voice is your victory.

Winning doesn't mean *never losing*. It means never losing sight of what matters most.

It's integrity. It's resilience. It's self-trust.

It's remembering that showing up for yourself is the boldest move you can make in a world that profits off your self-doubt.

And maybe—just maybe—that's the biggest win of all.

Final Word (For Now)

I'm not here to hand you a ribbon or a checklist.

I'm here to hand you a mirror.

I want you to look at yourself—really look—and recognize what you've already survived. The battles you've fought. The betrayals you've healed from. The losses you've carried. The strength it took to get out of bed some days. That's *winning*.

If you've lived through pain, loss, shame, failure, fear, addiction, disappointment, burnout, betrayal, or anything else that tried to break you … and you're still standing?

You've already won.

You are proof that resilience is real. You are evidence that miracles walk around in messy hair and worn-out shoes. You are the reason someone else might find the courage to try again.

So as you turn the pages of this book, I want you to do it with the understanding that you're not reading about other people's greatness—you're reconnecting with your own.

Let these stories remind you of what's possible. Let them wake up the sleeping giant inside you. Let them pull you out of your "not yet" and into your "right now."

And the next time someone doubts your greatness—or you doubt it yourself—smile and whisper what I've said to myself a thousand times:

"I'm wired to win. Watch me."

Because if this book does its job—and I believe it will—you won't just walk away inspired, you'll walk away ignited, with a fire in your gut, a spark in your soul, and a strategy in your back pocket.

This isn't motivation for a moment, this is transformation for a lifetime.

So go ahead. Flip the page. Start the chapter. Begin the comeback.

You're wired to win.

And the world is waiting.

SUZANNE EVANS

Suzanne Evans, the power behind Driven Inc., is a NY Times Best Selling Author of The Way You Do Anything Is the Way You Do Everything. She is a 5x INC 500/5000 recipient. Suzanne Evans went from secretary to seven-figure CEO and is now known as the "tell-it-like-it-is", no-fluff boss of business building. She provides support, consulting, and business development skills to entrepreneurs enrolled in her wealth and business-building programs.

Suzanne's "why" moment came in 2007, while working a day job behind the scenes on Broadway. As she looked over her credit card statements and realized it would take 21 years to pay off her debt, she decided the only way to create the life she wanted was for her to take immediate action. Suzanne opened up shop inside a Whole Foods Market. Literally. Emboldened by her ability to get clients in what was the least likely of places (between the bananas and tomatoes), she realized that her success in business would depend on her ability to master embarrassment, marketing and sales, and inspire clients to "share their mess" as a pathway to getting clients and making money.

www.DrivenInc.com

WIRED TO WIN

Marion Jones

I used to think being wired to win meant being the fastest. First across the finish line. First on the podium. First to prove everyone wrong.

Now I know better.

Winning isn't just about what the world sees. It's not the headline or the highlight reel. It's about how you show up when no one's watching. It's how you rise after you fall—especially when the fall breaks every piece of your public identity.

My story begins like so many others—with a dream. But mine also came with a prophecy.

I was just a little girl when I first heard it. My maternal grandfather worked in Guatemala. He had some extra quetzals in his pocket and decided to stop on the side of the road and get his fortune told. The woman proceeded to tell him, "Someone in your family will achieve greatness on another level."

At the time, it was just a sentence. A whisper on the wind told to my mother, who then, of course, shared it with me. But for my mom, it became a beacon. A reason to believe. A fire to pass down.

And she did.

My mom, also named Marion, was the first leg of the relay. She left Belize as a teenager, full of dreams and stubborn resolve. She worked hard and fought for everything—working long hours, commuting each day across Los Angeles to give my brother and me a chance at something better.

She didn't raise me to chase comfort. She raised me to run full steam ahead at my dreams.

And run I did.

Built for the Win

I didn't walk anywhere—I sprinted. Even as a kid, I had this energy that could barely be contained. If there was a ball, I chased it. If there was a finish line, I crossed it. Sometimes I didn't even wait for the start gun—I just went. And having an older brother to push the pace and challenge me even more certainly helped.

Ira, my stepfather, came into my life when I was five. A retired Navy cook with a quiet strength and deep love for sports, he gave me a foundation I didn't even know I needed. When he died suddenly when I was ten, that foundation cracked—and something inside me hardened.

I turned to sports with a new intensity. Every lap was therapy. Every race was a declaration. I didn't have the language back then, but I was translating grief into grit. Pain into power. Loss into momentum.

I watched the 1984 Olympics that summer with wide eyes, a chalkboard in my room meant for summer school assignments. I scrawled one sentence across it: "I will be an Olympic champion."

Not *I hope*. Not *maybe*.

I will.

That wasn't ego. That was wiring.

Winning on Paper

I became known for what I could do with my body. Fast. Powerful. Explosive. Whether it was soccer, gymnastics, basketball, or track, I rose through the ranks with speed and focus that didn't leave much room for doubt.

At UNC, I played point guard and helped my team win a national championship my freshman year. I led on the court, and I flew on the track. I had dreams of five gold medals at the 2000 Sydney Olympics, and I trained with that singular vision every day.

When I told a reporter years earlier I'd win five medals, it wasn't a boast. It was a blueprint. I believed it. I had trained for it. I was wired to manifest it.

And in Sydney, I almost did.

Three golds. Two bronze. And for a brief moment, I stood on top of the world—smiling, unshakable, the picture of success.

The world saw victory.

What they didn't see was the cost.

Cracks in the Medal

My then-husband was also in Sydney. His career was collapsing under doping violations. I defended him publicly, even as my doubts grew in private. The truth is, I didn't just want to believe in him—I needed to. Because if he was guilty … what did that say about me?

I was in control on the track, but off the track, everything felt slippery. Contracts. Coaches. Agents. When people depend on your success for their paycheck, you start to lose sight of who's really in your corner.

After I divorced, I took control of my own career. I fired people. Hired new ones. Managed my training. It felt good—empowering, even—but I was still living in a world built on the perception of perfection. And I knew, deep down, that perception couldn't hold.

The rumors were constant.

And eventually, they caught up to me.

The Fall

In 2007, I stood in front of a judge and confessed: I lied to federal prosecutors. I never knowingly used performance enhancing drugs but when confronted by the feds, I lied about what I had been given, and it caught up to me ... BIG TIME!

I had made decisions—trusted people I shouldn't have, and looked the other way when the stakes were too high to face the truth head-on.

The fallout was fast and devastating.

Medals: gone.
Sponsorships: gone.
Reputation: shattered.

But what hurt most wasn't the headlines. It was facing myself. I wasn't the person I thought I was. I had spent so many years running away from that truth, I didn't recognize the version of me who finally had to stop.

When I was sentenced to six months in prison, I remember thinking, *This is it. This is the bottom.*

And in many ways, it was. But that bottom gave me something I never had before: silence. Stillness. A forced reckoning.

Inside those walls, I wasn't a champion. I wasn't a star. I was just Marion.

And for the first time in my life … that was enough.

The Real Race Begins

Prison changed me—not because of the punishment, but because of the clarity.

It stripped away everything I used to think made me valuable: medals, titles, applause. All I had left was me.

And what I discovered in that quiet was that real winning doesn't happen in the spotlight. It happens in the dark. When no one is watching. When the world has turned its back, you have to decide— are you going to rise, or are you going to retreat?

When I got out, I had no PR team. No contracts. No parade.

But I had a purpose.

I started speaking to young athletes. Not to warn them, but to equip them. To show them that integrity matters. That chasing a dream at all costs isn't winning—it's erasure. And that there's always a way back, if you're willing to tell the truth.

And more than anything, I had to start doing the inner work. Not the physical training I'd mastered as an athlete—but the emotional training I'd avoided for years. Therapy. Stillness. Learning to forgive myself. Learning to breathe without a stopwatch. Those were actually the most difficult laps to run, but they were essential. And every time I spoke my truth—whether to students, athletes, or my own children—I ran a little farther into freedom.

Wired Differently Now

Today, I'm a mother. A partner. A woman still running—but with a different fuel and purpose.

I'm in a loving, committed relationship with my partner, and I proudly identify as a lesbian. That journey—of identity, truth, and self-love—has been its own marathon, one I wasn't ready to run in my twenties. But now, I run it with joy and pride.

Motherhood gave me perspective. My kids don't care about Olympic stats. They care about bedtime stories. About presence. About love.

And that love anchored me during some of the hardest years of my life.

I've rebuilt slowly. Intentionally. I still speak. I still run. I still lift weights. But the person you see now isn't built on performance—she's built on truth.

Now, I define success differently. It's no longer about being on the cover of a magazine. It's about how I show up in my relationships. How I model resilience for my children. How I help others unlock the parts of themselves that have been buried under shame or fear.

Every day, I work to align with my values—authenticity, courage, integrity. That's how I measure victory now. And let me tell you, some days I win. Some days I fall short. But I always show up. That, to me, is what it means to still be wired to win.

The Strategy

So, what does it mean to be wired to win?

It's not about being first. It's not about being flawless. It's not about pretending you're invincible.

It's about:

— Knowing yourself even when the world defines you by your worst day.
— Telling the truth even when it costs you everything.
— Falling with grace and getting back up with purpose.
— Choosing integrity over image, peace over praise.

Winning isn't the medal.

It's the mindset.

It's the moment you decide your worth isn't tied to performance—but to presence.

It's what you do in the spaces between the victories that defines you. How you live when no one's clapping. How you show up for your kids, your partner, your future, and yourself.

It's also about recognizing that the finish line keeps moving—and that's okay. Winning is no longer a static goal for me. It's a way of living. It's embedded in my routines, in my decisions, in the courage to choose growth over comfort.

It's in how I move forward—not despite my past, but because I've made peace with it. My wiring hasn't changed—it's just been rerouted. It's no longer fueled by fear of failure or the need for validation. Now, it's fueled by truth, faith, and the unwavering belief that I was built not just to win—but to evolve.

That's the strategy.
That's the work.
That's what I wish someone had told me when I was nine years old, writing on my chalkboard.

You don't win because you're fast.

You win because you know who you are, even when everything's been taken away.

I've been the fastest woman in the world.

I've also been a mother, daughter, partner, and truth-teller.

And if I had to choose?

I'd take this version of winning—every single time.

MARION JONES

Marion Jones is a five-time Olympic medalist and NCAA basketball champion, who became one of the most celebrated athletes in the world. Today, she is a speaker, mentor, and mother (and recently competed on Season 3 of *Special Forces: The World's Toughest Test*), using her story to teach resilience, integrity, and the power of starting over.

www.MarionJones.com

TRAINED TO MANAGE. BUILT TO LEAD. THE SHIFT THEY NEVER TAUGHT YOU, BUT YOU'RE READY FOR

Jill K. Adams

"Unhook the plow."

That's what my dad used to yell at me. Not while I worked the land, though I've spent plenty of time in soybeans, picking weeds. He'd shout it from the stands during my softball games, as I launched toward first base.

"UNHOOK THE PLOW, JILL!"

To outsiders, it probably sounded bizarre. Who yells farm talk at a ball field? But I knew exactly what he meant. If a tractor is pulling the plow, it can only go so fast. It's dragging weight. Let it go, and it flies.

He wasn't yelling at me to try harder. He was telling me to release, stop overthinking, and let go of invisible burdens: fear, doubt, perfectionism, pressure, expectation.

That phrase stuck with me long after the final inning.

Just like that tractor, leaders often carry invisible weight that slows us down. Until we unhook the plow, we can't lead with the clarity and energy our teams need.

Because here's the truth: Most of us, especially high-performing leaders, are still pulling a plow.

Maybe you are, too.

You wake up early. Show up strong. Lead meetings, solve problems, steer the ship. You're holding it together. You're managing.

And yet, it feels heavy.

Your team might be coasting; doing what's required but missing the spark. You're stuck in the same conversations, facing resistance, paddling upstream.

You're tired. Frustrated. Quietly wondering if this is really the dream you signed up for.

No one warns you that leadership, while rewarding, can be profoundly lonely.

You're squeezed between pressure from above and pushback from below. Trying to motivate, direct, inspire, and in the chaos, you realize you're surviving, not leading.

Let me say this clearly: This is not all there is. But something has to shift.

Not your team. Not your org chart. You.

Because managing is like driving with one foot on the gas and one on the brake. You'll move, but it'll take twice the effort, and you'll burn out before you ever arrive.

The game changes when you shift from managing to coaching. When you stop controlling and start cultivating. When you stop fixing and start unlocking.

That's when transformation happens. That's when you unhook the plow.

Not just for yourself, but for everyone who looks to you for leadership.

Over the past decade, I've helped hundreds of high-performing leaders make this move. What changes everything isn't doing more; it's shifting how you show up.

I call this your Signature Shift.

It's the pivotal move every high-performing leader must make: away from managing tasks and toward unlocking people. It's called your Signature Shift because the way you do it is personal. Unrepeatable. Yours.

But the impact? That's universal.

Here's how to make it happen:

—

Shift One: Trust Like You Mean It

Trust is the soil every other shift grows from. Without it, nothing else takes root. Once trust is established, the next step is to deepen it, and that starts with how you listen.

If your leadership is a house, trust is the foundation. No trust, no structure.

And I'm not talking about corporate poster trust. I mean real-deal, show-up-as-you-are trust.

That kind of trust isn't built in breakout rooms or team-building retreats. It's built in the micro moments.

I coached a leader once who felt her team was disengaged. Strong performers, robotic energy. People showed up, did their jobs, and stayed quiet.

So we started small. She began scheduling informal one-on-ones, not for status updates, but for human connection. She asked about weekends. Favorite meals. Personal goals.

Slowly, something shifted: walls dropped, energy returned, trust took root.

Soon her team was bringing fresh ideas, solving problems proactively, and pushing the work forward without her constant oversight.

They didn't feel managed. They felt seen.

And people who feel seen will run through walls for you.

Trust isn't soft. It's strategy.

The Signature Shift Cue: Schedule one casual, non-work check-in: no agenda. Just connect. Then ask: What's one small action you can take to show your team you trust them?

—

Shift Two: Listen Like It Matters

Most leaders think they're good listeners. They nod. Maintain eye contact. Don't interrupt.

But real listening, the coaching kind, is different.

It means being fully present.

It means hearing the unsaid. The tension behind the words. The need under the complaint.

I had a client who stopped jumping in with quick fixes during meetings and instead started asking real questions: "Can you say more?" "What do you think we should try?" "What feels like the root issue here?"

And then she held space.

At first, it felt awkward. She told me, "Jill, I wanted to fill the silence with answers."

But over time? Her team filled it with brilliance.

Ideas got better. Collaboration deepened. They even began challenging each other and her.

Because when leaders listen, people lean in.

Active listening doesn't just build trust. It builds momentum.

It tells your team: This isn't a monologue. This is a partnership.

Let this week be your listening lab. Ask one open-ended question, and when the silence hits, let it stretch. Resist the urge to fill it. Let it teach you. Where in your leadership could listening, not solving, create the biggest shift?

—

Shift Three: Let Go of Every Decision

One of the hardest truths for high achievers to swallow:

You are the bottleneck.

You've built your brand on being the go-to person. The one who knows. The one who gets it done.

But if every decision flows through you, you're not leading; you're gatekeeping.

I worked with a marketing director who was beloved and buried. Every campaign, every email, every decision, she was looped in.

We created "zones of ownership" for her team. Each person got a lane, with clear boundaries. Inside that lane? They led.

She backed off. They stepped up.

Confidence grew. Creativity exploded. And she finally had breathing room to think, plan, lead.

Delegation isn't abdication; it's multiplication.

And when people know you trust them to own it, they'll rise to match it.

LEADER TAKEAWAY Action: Choose one decision you're holding that someone else could own. Hand it off with clear context and full trust. Where are you holding onto too tightly, and what could shift if you released it?

—

Shift Four: Make Feedback Normal

When you delegate decisions, you create space for growth. And feedback is the fuel that drives that growth.

Most people treat feedback like a dentist visit: necessary but painful.

Why? Because we've made it awkward, inconsistent, and often weaponized.

But feedback done right is fuel.

One team I worked with created a weekly rhythm called Feedback Fridays. Each person gave one piece of praise and one nudge for growth. Yes, it was clunky at first. But within months, it became the heartbeat of their culture.

No more tiptoeing. No more sugarcoating. Just honest, human conversation.

Feedback doesn't have to be formal. It just has to be frequent and real.

Say what you see. Say it with care. Say it until it becomes the norm, not a nerve-wracker.

Here's your challenge: Give one piece of honest, kind feedback and ask for one in return. Let it be normal, not dramatic. Pause and reflect: What kind of feedback culture are you modeling, and what shift would happen if you normalized real talk?

—

Shift Five: Change Your Role, Not Just Your Mindset

This is where it all locks in.

You are not the hero. You are the guide.

Coaching is not hand-holding. It's high-impact leadership.

It means you stop being the source of all answers and start being the catalyst for all growth.

You don't control outcomes. You cultivate potential.

This shift is subtle, but seismic.

It turns your role from commander to conductor, from hustler to cultivator.

And when you lead this way, people don't just follow you. They lead themselves.

That's how you scale impact. That's how you build legacy.

The Signature Shift Cue: In your next meeting, don't lead. Facilitate. Ask instead of answer. Step back and let others rise. Reflect on this: Are you building leaders or just managing outcomes?

—

Now I want to take you back to one of the scariest and most transformative experiences of my life.

Now, let's go to the edge, literally.

I went skydiving.

I am not a thrill-seeker. I am a "hold the ladder" kind of woman. Heights are not my jam. When we were kids, my twin sister would climb on roofs with my dad. I made sandwiches. Safe. Steady. Firmly grounded.

But something whispered: Be brave.

So I booked the jump. Drove two hours, heart pounding.

On that drive, I called people I love: my parents, siblings, kids. Said things I hadn't taken time to say. Laughed. Cried. Remembered what matters.

When I arrived, I felt calm. Centered. Even the instructor said, "You seem way too relaxed for a first-timer."

And I was.

Until I was halfway out of the plane.

Hanging in the open doorway, wind rushing past me, it hit.

What I expected to feel, absolute terror, I didn't. I felt excited. WHAT?! That moment shocked me. But when the countdown ended and I leapt, something else cracked open.

It only took two seconds of courage.

And instead of fear, I found trust.

Trust in the instructor. The parachute. The process. Myself.

And the view? Breathtaking.

The fall was free. The silence was sacred. And the landing, smooth.

That day taught me something I didn't expect:

Courage opens the door. But trust carries you through.

That's leadership, too.

Just like I had to trust the instructor and the parachute, leaders must trust their teams and the systems they've built. It's not about being fearless; it's about having the courage to let go.

So if you're reading this and feeling stuck, frustrated, unseen, or unsure …

If your team is stalled, or your energy is drained, or your joy is gone …

This is *your* whisper.

Your invitation to stop dragging the weight and start rising into a new way of leading.

Unhook the plow. Make the shift. Coach with curiosity. Lead with trust.

Start with one small action today.

Leadership isn't about doing it all; it's about unlocking potential in yourself and others.

And when you do that?

You give yourself permission to fly.

JILL ADAMS

Jill Adams is the trusted advisor high-performing leaders call when they're ready to stop managing and start leading with purpose, clarity, and real impact. Farm-raised and boardroom-tested, she brings over two decades of executive leadership in sales, culture strategy, and leadership development.

A Certified High Performance Coach™, keynote speaker, and creator of the Signature Shifts framework, Jill has worked with Fortune-level teams, the State of Minnesota, and senior leaders across energy, finance, and healthcare.

She helps leadership teams ditch burnout and outdated management models to build teams that perform, cultures that last, and clarity that cuts through the noise.

www.Jill-Adams.com

DARE TO DREAM: CREATE THE LIFE YOU WANT

Charlotte Bishop

You walk up to a new house.

From the outside, it looks promising—fresh paint, new windows, a welcoming front door. But the moment you step inside, the promise vanishes. The door opens into a blank space—no floor, a hallway that dead-ends into a wall, a staircase that goes up …stops at a blank wall. The kitchen is beautiful, but there's no way to reach it from the room where you are standing. It's all confusing …disjointed … ridiculous.

You ask the builder, "What is this?"

And they shrug and say, "We didn't get a blueprint. We just kind of figured it out as we went along."

You'd probably laugh …or stare in disbelief. No one builds a house that way …or do they?

Here's the uncomfortable truth: Most people build their lives that way, especially the second half …the part where the stairs went up but hit a blank wall.

We put so much thought and effort into the early chapters. There are lots of goals and landmarks for a successful career: a degree, a job in our field of choice, a relationship, a family, even a financial account for retirement, and then …then WHAT? We chase goals, meet deadlines, do what's expected. We plan every step …until we don't.

When it comes to the chapter after all that—the one where we finally get to focus on ourselves—most of us have no plan at all.

We assume we'll "figure it out." We'll get there, and something will click. But I've seen too many people arrive at that moment—retirement, reinvention, whatever you want to call it—and feel disappointed. Disoriented. Like they woke up in a life that doesn't quite fit. One of my family doesn't say he's retired; he says he's "unemployed." He had the money, but no plan. Most people fit that profile. Still another is so overwhelmed with caregiving responsibilities, she feels invisible and exhausted wondering what happened to *her* life.

Then they look around at friends who are thriving …traveling, creating, connecting …and wonder, *Why does their life look so good? Why doesn't mine feel like that?*

PLAN

The answer isn't luck or privilege or some perfect set of circumstances.

It's planning. It's intention. It's the result of a blueprint that was actually drawn and followed. It may require a crew to build, but the Blueprint comes first.

I believe the second half of life can absolutely outperform the first. But that doesn't happen by accident. It happens by design.

It begins with something we're not often encouraged to do: *DREAM*

Not vague, someday pipe dreams. I mean vivid, grounded, deeply personal dreams. The kind you can feel. The kind that helps you remember who you really are underneath the roles, responsibilities, and routines. The kind of dreams that help you live with intention, joy, and meaning. Dreams that are uniquely, deliciously yours.

Let me walk you through it.

Close your eyes. Take a breath. Imagine yourself at seventy. It's not a birthday. Not a holiday. Just an ordinary day. You wake up. What's around you? Sunlight pouring in through a window? A favorite blanket? A quiet room? A joyful one? Who's nearby? A partner? A pet? Silence?

Now, imagine breakfast. What are you eating? What do you hear in the background? Music? Birds? Laughter? What are you looking forward to? A walk? A book? A visit with someone you love?

How does this day feel?

That image—that perfectly ordinary, yet beautiful day—isn't just fantasy. It's insight. It's a direction. It's what your future could look like, if you choose to design it, rather than just waiting for it to happen.

And that's what I help people do.

As a retirement lifestyle coach, I work with people from their forties to their eighties, ready to start thinking differently about what comes next. Some are still in the thick of work and family, but they know they want something more, not yet realizing that it's their life to create, not a subway platform where they're waiting to board the train. Some are approaching retirement and craving clarity. Others are already in retirement and are shocked to find they feel... a little lost. Still others are caring for a loved one and wonder: "What about me? What happened to *my* life?"

Wherever you are on your path, it's not too late or too early to draft your blueprint.

I call it the Live Well Blueprint^{sm}, and it's rooted in more than theory. It draws from my background as a counselor and vocational coach. And honestly? From the **ten** homes I've personally renovated. I know what it takes to look at something unfinished, outdated, or stuck—and imagine what it could be. I roll up my sleeves and make it happen.

That's what I want to do for you.

Because you're standing in front of the next twenty, thirty, even forty years of your life. It's time to stop winging it—and start designing it.

KNOW YOUR NUMBERS

So how do you start designing the second half of your life, especially if no one has ever shown you how?

It begins with something simple, but surprisingly hard: giving yourself permission to *DREAM*.

We don't realize how early we learn to shrink ourselves. To be practical, responsible. To make choices that keep everyone else comfortable, even if we stay stuck—especially women. We become experts at being dependable, needed, efficient. We lose sight of the parts of us that are curious, restless, creative, ALIVE.

And then one day, the roles begin to shift, the job is winding down. The kids are grown. A loved one has a health crisis. You realize life is changing. The routine gets quieter. And in the stillness, there's this subtle ache …a whisper that says, *What now?*

That's not a crisis. It's an opportunity …an opening.

Walk through it, reconnect with your desires, not what other people expect from you. What's your dream, what's your vision?

DREAM

When I work with clients, I often begin with a simple dream exercise: Describe your perfect average day. Not the bucket list. Not the big milestone moments. Just a regular Tuesday that feels like it's yours by design.

People initially struggle. They list tasks, responsibilities. But the real landscape emerges. Mornings with space. Work that feels meaningful …or perhaps no work at all. Time to think. Time to create.

That picture becomes the foundation. From there, we build the Blueprint.

But dreams don't come to life without structure. That takes planning.

Planning is not about restriction; it's about freedom. The freedom to make choices from a place of clarity instead of fear. To know when you can say yes, and when you can let go.

And part of that means knowing your numbers.

Too often, people reach midlife or retirement without any real grasp of their financial picture. They either overestimate and delay joy, or underestimate and feel anxious. Both lead to lives lived smaller than necessary.

Knowing your numbers doesn't mean obsessing over spreadsheets. It means understanding what it costs to live the life you want, and making sure the decisions you make now support that future.

Whether you're five years from retirement or fifteen, it's worth sitting down with a planner who gets it …someone who understands that money is not just math. It's *freedom fuel*. It's what lets you book the trip, take the class, leave the job, or build the thing you've been dreaming of.

But even with a clear vision and a strong plan, there's one thing that will still try to hold you back: fear. Fear is sneaky. It doesn't always show up as panic or dread. Sometimes it's just a vague hesitation. A habit of putting things off. A voice that whispers, *Maybe next year,* or *Who do you think you are to want that?*

I've heard those voices, too. So have all my clients. But here's the truth:

Fear doesn't mean stop. It means pay attention.

It means something important is on the other side of that discomfort.

So what do we do?

We don't wait; we take steps, even if they're baby steps. We move—one step at a time.

Maybe it's calling the financial planner. Maybe it's reflective journaling or researching a city you've dreamed of calling home, signing up for that dance class, painting workshop, book club, or travel.

Even small steps make the dream more real.

They build momentum, clarity, and confidence.

They remind you that you're not stuck, you're not too late. It's how we build the Blueprint for the life we want to live, not the one we were handed.

You've imagined the life, considered the steps, made the plan.

Now comes the most important part: choosing to begin.

Not next year. Not when everything is figured out. Not when you feel more confident or less afraid.

Now.

Because this life you want won't build itself. It's your vision.

And if you don't design it, someone else will.

It can feel overwhelming, but the truth is, designing your life isn't about doing everything at once. It's about choosing to live *on purpose.* To align your days with what matters, stop drifting through years and start directing them.

You're not behind. You're not late. You're exactly where you need to be to take the next step.

So dream bigger. Plan wisely. Move confidently.

Ask for help. Let go of the story that your best days are behind you …they're waiting for you.

I've worked with people who thought their stories were winding down, only to discover they were at the first page of their most fulfilling chapter yet. They're moving from restless to rooted, from burned out to feeling renewed, from uncertain to clear.

And every time, it began with one decision: I'm not going to live by default anymore. I'm going to live by my designs, my decisions.

Reclaim what matters, build your life with your Blueprint, your values, your energy, your joy. Your dreams. Because your second half? It isn't a fade-out. It's a masterpiece waiting to be crafted. And when you do?

I'll be here …T-square in hand, ready to help you bring your Blueprint to life.

CHARLOTTE BISHOP

Charlotte Bishop is a certified Aging Life Care Professional® and creator of Live Well Blueprint℠, a customized planning approach for those who refuse to settle for just "OK" in life's next chapter. With over 35 years of experience, she combines Retirement Lifestyle Coaching with expert Care Management to help clients design vibrant futures or navigate health crises—before choices disappear. Too many wait and wonder where the years went. Charlotte urges: don't drift – dare to dream. With a clear vision and compassionate guidance, her clients reclaim purpose, joy, and possibility—and create a life they love for the next 20, 30, even 40 years.

www.CreativeCareManagement.com

WINNING STARTS AT HOME: THE ROOT OF WHAT'S HOLDING YOU BACK

Heidi M. Bolyard

Let's just start with the awkward truth: I spend a lot of time with couples in their bedrooms.

That usually gets a laugh, but I mean it in the most professional way possible. As a residential architect, no matter where we begin a home consultation, the front porch, the mudroom, or the kitchen island, we almost always end up in the primary bedroom. It's uncanny.

It's not because I steer them there. It's because that's where people let their guard down. That's where the polite small talk fades and the real conversations begin. Where people stop commenting on storage space and start whispering what they're really searching for:

"I just want to walk in the door and not feel stressed."
"We're not using half the rooms in our home, so we avoid them."
"This home no longer works for our family."

I've learned that people often walk through their homes quietly tolerating things for years, storage that never quite works, a layout that adds stress, or rooms that sit unused, like forgotten corners of their life. It's only when they say it out loud, often for the first time, that they begin to realize: It's not just the house that needs to change.

31

It's how they feel in it. And that moment of realization? That's the real starting line.

That's when the shift begins, not in the floor plan but in the feeling. When the conversation moves from square footage to something more personal.

From how the house looks, to how it actually functions.

And that's where *you* come in.

When I talk about creating a home that truly supports you, I'm not just speaking as an architect, I'm speaking as someone who's been obsessed with design since before she could tie her own shoes.

When I was three years old, I was already designing houses.

In secret.

Like a tiny, rogue HGTV host with crayons and zero adult supervision. Not with Legos or Lincoln Logs, nope, I drew on the walls … underneath my bed. Because obviously, that's where all great architects start.

Years later, when we moved out of that house, my parents pulled the bed away from the wall and found it; my first portfolio with little floor plans, strange symbols, letters and logos. It looked like hieroglyphics in a cave channeled by a toddler.

The wildest part? My mom didn't think to mention it to me until a few years ago. I was like, "You waited almost fifty years to tell me my first masterpiece was hiding under my bed?" Honestly, it explained a lot.

Because now, decades later, I get paid to do that very thing, just with cleaner lines. Sometimes sitting at my desk, Sharpie in hand, sketching elevations, I think, *Is this a real career or a very elaborate scam I accidentally pulled off?*

Since 2001, I've been designing dream homes, renovations, and even the occasional custom doghouse. What I've learned is this: Most homes already hold the potential for greatness. The problem isn't usually square footage or style, it's clarity.

Because if your home doesn't reflect how you live or want to feel, it quietly works against you.

But when your space starts to align with your rhythms, values, and energy, everything shifts. That's when your home stops holding you back and starts helping you move forward.

After working with nearly a thousand families, I've realized we are designing our homes backward.

We decorate our homes based on what we *see*: Pinterest boards, HGTV shows, glossy home magazines. We scroll, screenshot, and pin until we've pieced together something that looks "right." But underneath it all, something feels … off.

We're designing for approval, not alignment.

In fact, a recent study found that 67 percent of homeowners admitted to choosing design elements simply because they saw it online, even if it didn't reflect their taste or personality.

And if we're being really honest, a lot of us are still trying to keep up with the Joneses.

Let me tell you something about the Joneses.

They're broke. They're stressed. And they hate their kitchen backsplash.

We spend thousands of dollars trying to recreate someone else's dream, without ever asking: *How do I want this space to feel?*

And so, we end up with homes that look great, but don't feel right to us. Homes that are visually styled but emotionally disconnected. Homes that quietly keep us from living our best life.

When you design from the inside out, when you anchor your space in your values, memories, and emotions, your home becomes more than stylish.

It becomes sacred.

It becomes yours.

For example, in my dining room, I have a goat.

No, not a real goat. He's ceramic and doesn't eat houseplants. Very low maintenance.

This little guy is a total conversation starter. People walk in, point, and say, "What's with the goat?"

I smile and say, "Funny you should ask."

See, when I was young, I had a friend who always teased me for having the name Heidi. She'd say, "Where are your goats, Heidi? Are they grazing out back?"

It became a running joke. Decades later, that goat reminds me of her. Of that season of life. Of the laughter we shared.

He also happens to pair really well with a glass of red wine.

And in my kitchen? A tiny Hummel figurine, one of those wide-eyed German children. Definitely not trending on any design blog. But my grandmother had about a hundred of them. And when I see that little figurine, I feel like she's right there with me, humming a tune while I cook.

That's what I love helping people do, not just decorate with style, but infuse their spaces with meaning and memory. Because that's what makes it home.

*   *   *

Over time, I realized most people don't know how to create that kind of connection in their homes. They know what looks good on Instagram. They know what their neighbor's new renovation looks like, but they don't know what *they* want. Not really.

So, I created a tool to help. It's called the **Home Transformation Blueprint**. Think of it like guided self-discovery for your living room or therapy for your walls.

Here's how it works: You walk into a room, any room, and ask ten simple but powerful questions. Questions like:

- *How does this space make me feel?*
- *What's actually working in this space?*
- *What's not, and why?*
- *Where do I feel most comfortable in my home?*
- *What's missing that I wish I had?*

It's a process designed to pull the truth out of you. Not just about your home, but about your life. And once you start answering these questions, the design answers start to show up, too.

What does this look like in real life?

One family came to me with a surprisingly emotional challenge, their mornings were a daily battle. The entry had become a dumping zone, and the kitchen, a bottleneck. Everyone rushing around, tripping on backpacks and stumbling over each other. By the time they left the house at 8 a.m., they were all exhausted.

They didn't need more space, just a better system, and a better layout to support it. We reworked the floor plan to carve out a mudroom just inside the garage entry. The new space allowed for cubbies for each kid, coat hooks, a charging station for tech, and a bench for putting shoes on.

That simple shift transformed their mornings. There was calm, routine, and even laughter.

Environmental psychology backs this up, too. The spaces we inhabit directly affect our emotional health. Our mood. Our stress levels. Even our immune system. Design isn't just visual, it's energetic. It shapes how we feel and how we function.

Another couple came to me frustrated with their kitchen. "We trip over each other," they said. "It's like the house is working against us." In many ways, it was.

The kitchen layout hadn't changed since the nineties. Three kids, a love of cooking, and a revolving door of neighbors and friends; the space couldn't keep up.

We reimagined the entire flow by opening a wall and rotating the island. We adjusted the circulation so people could gather without getting in the way. Suddenly, their kitchen wasn't just functional, it was magnetic.

When you start to see things differently:

A hallway becomes a gallery of memories.
A den becomes a place of fun and laughter.
A quirky layout becomes the rhythm that fits real life.

Our homes don't just hold our things; they hold our stories. And sometimes, all it takes to begin shifting that story is one question, one honest moment, or one reimagined room.

What changed in both of these homes wasn't just the layout. It was the clarity.

The truth is your home is a mirror. And when it's not aligned with your life, it doesn't just feel off. *It is off.*

It reflects how you move through the world. It amplifies your stress or your peace. It can reinforce old patterns or create space for new ones.

*　*　*

That little girl sketching on the wall under her bed?

She wasn't trying to impress anyone. She wasn't worried about resale value or trending colors. She just wanted to create something that felt right.

I didn't know then what I was doing. It just made me feel alive.

So here's your invitation:

Start with one question. Walk into a room, maybe the one you avoid the most, and ask yourself: *What would this space look like if it truly reflected me?*

Not your mom.
Not HGTV.
Not the algorithm.
You.

And maybe, just maybe, add a goat.

Because sometimes the smallest, weirdest things tell the best stories.

This is how transformation begins. Not with a sledgehammer, but with a shift in perspective.

Because when your home reflects your values, supports your routines, and holds your life with intention, everything gets easier.

That's not just good design.

And the best part?
You just have to begin, right where you are.
At home.

And that? That's where winning truly begins.

HEIDI M. BOLYARD

Heidi Bolyard is a residential architect, speaker, and the founder of Simplified Living Architecture. Since 2000, she's helped nearly a thousand families eliminate frustration in their homes by designing spaces that reflect how they truly live, bringing more calm, clarity, and joy into everyday life. Specializing in custom homes and whole-house renovations, Heidi creates spaces that support connection, ease, and meaningful living. Known for her intuitive process and deep listening, she believes that a well-designed home isn't just beautiful, it's life-changing. Heidi is a Registered Architect in Ohio and Florida, and a LEED BD+C Accredited Professional. Learn more at www.gettingbackhome.com.

www.GettingBackHome.com

TALK IS CHEAP: WHY MOST ENTREPRENEURS FAIL ON STAGE AND WHAT TO DO INSTEAD

Dannella Burnett

Let me start with a little surprise.

I'm not here to talk about *speaking*.

Now, that might sound odd coming from someone who runs a company called Speakers Need to Speak. You're probably thinking, *Dannella, come on. That's your thing!*

But stay with me here.

Because what I want to talk about is *talking*.

Yes, talking. The thing most people are doing right now. And if that stings a little, good! That means we're getting somewhere. See, there's a big difference between talking and speaking. And once you understand it, everything changes.

Talking is what happens when you get up and deliver your message without intention. No game plan. No strategy. Just words. It might be powerful, heartfelt, even funny. But if there's no purpose behind it? It's noise.

Speaking, on the other hand, *real* speaking, is calculated, intentional, and profitable. It's about getting on the right stage, in front of the right people, with the right message and the right offer. It's about visibility that converts. Impact that pays. Words that *work and hit their mark*.

Talking is cheap. Speaking pays the bills. Speaking will grow your bank account.

Here's the kicker: Most people already *know* they should be speaking. You've heard it. You've probably told someone else. "You need to get out there. Get visible. Share your message." You know the power of stages. You know, speaking changes businesses.

So you commit.

You write the talk. You gather the stories. You obsess over the transitions. You pour your heart into your message, into your slides, into your performance. You practice. You perfect. You even go shopping: new shoes, new lipstick, the works. You're ready.

Except … you're not.

Because soon reality hits. You don't know where to speak. Or you find a gig, but it's the *wrong* one. Wrong crowd. Wrong setting. No offer. Or the offer's off. Or the follow-up fizzles. Either way, you end up doing all this work and getting nothing from it.

And suddenly, you're just talking again. Not speaking. Talking.

That's the gap. And it's where so many passionate, talented, brilliant entrepreneurs get stuck.

That's where I come in.

My job, my mission, is to help you close that gap. To help you stop spinning your wheels and start building real momentum. I put speakers on stages around the world. And I don't just get them booked, I help them *maximize* those moments. I help them build strategies that make those stages work for them.

But before I did any of that?

I met Julia Child.

Okay, not in person. I was nine. She was on TV. But in that moment, I was hooked. She had this energy, this confidence, this magnetic quality that made you just lean in. She made an omelet and somehow made it feel like theater. I thought I loved the food. So I started cooking.

And cooking.

The infamous "Death by Chocolate" Thanksgiving happened not long after. Eight different varieties of chocolate in one heavy, carb-loaded, nap-inducing chocolate dessert. For Thanksgiving ... the one meal that doesn't need heavy. One very nauseated family. But I was determined. I went to culinary school. Competed internationally. Won medals. Opened a catering business. Hosted giant events. Closed down four city blocks for Oktoberfest.

And then one day, I realized something embarrassing that was hard to admit to myself..

I didn't want to cook for others anymore.

I loved the *experience* of food. I loved restaurants, presentation, and the *moment* of eating. But the prep? The chaos? The stress? Not for me anymore.

So what had captivated me about Julia Child?

It wasn't the food. It was the *teaching*. It was the way she *invited* us into the kitchen. She didn't just cook, she coached. She showed us the tools, the ingredients, the traps, the tricks. She made it *possible* for us to do what she did.

She guided people from being cooks to being chefs.

And that's exactly what I do. I help people go from being talkers to speakers.

It's the same recipe. You just change the ingredients.

Speaking is like cooking. You need the right prep, the right tools, the right stage, and the right audience. And once you get those things in place? You can create something people remember. Something that moves them.

So let's dig into what you actually need.

First: Not all gigs are created equal.

I see too many people chasing *any* opportunity. If there's a mic, they say yes. If there's a stage, they're on it. And I get it, you're hungry, you're motivated. But without a strategy? You're just exhausting yourself.

There are three types of gigs: paid before, paid during, and paid after.

Paid before: This is when you get booked by an organization to deliver a keynote. You're hired. You're paid. These are amazing and competitive. They require strong positioning and a standout message. You must show the value to the organization writing the check, not just value for the audience. These are more work to get, but absolutely possible.

Paid during: This is where you sell from the stage. You make an offer, and your talk sets the stage for that offer to land. Whether it's a program, a product, or a call, this is where conversion happens in real time, and you get paid in real time!

Paid after: These are lead-gen stages. Podcasts, summits, workshops, and opportunities where your focus is on collecting leads. Offering value and inviting people into your world. Think downloadable guides, opt-ins, email list growth, and continuing the conversation from the stage to a sales call.

Each of these has its own rhythm. Its own strategy. You need to know which one you're stepping into—and how to show up for it.

Because if you walk into a lead-gen gig and try to pitch a high-ticket offer without warming people up? It's going to fall flat. You're not wrong, you're just misaligned.

I had a client once, who was thrilled because she booked forty podcasts in forty days. Incredible, right? Except only five of those podcasts actually served her target audience. The rest? Complete mismatches. She was about to pour hours of effort into rooms full of people who would never become clients.

That's what happens when you chase opportunities without a filter.

So let's talk about how to find the *right* gigs.

You don't need to be famous. You need to be intentional.

Start with your network. Who do you already know? Who's already seen your brilliance? Those warm leads are often the easiest stages to land.

Next, scan your calendar. What events have you attended recently? Reach out to the organizers. Thank them for the experience. Ask how they choose speakers. You'd be surprised how often people overlook this. Use your past calendar to fill your future speaking gigs.

Then look at collaborations. Who serves your audience in a non-competitive way? Can you host a joint event? Do a stage swap? Create something together?

Social media is another treasure chest, but only if you treat it like a search engine, not a slot machine. Facebook groups, LinkedIn threads, for example, offer real opportunities, if you actually *look*.

And finally: the Google method. I teach the S.A.A.L.E. formula: Speaking Opportunities, Audience Description #1, Audience Description #2, Location, & Event type. Mix those terms in different combinations, and you'll uncover gold. It's not hard. It's just a habit.

But, and I can't stress this enough, none of that matters, if you're not *ready*.

Event producers want to say yes. But you have to make it easy.

Google yourself. What comes up? Is it polished, recent, and relevant? Or are you still showing up as your 2009 blog post about homemade lasagna?

Get yourself a reel or at least a clip. Show you can hold a room. And get your assets in order: a clean bio, a decent headshot, a one-sheet that actually reflects your work.

And yes, have a lead magnet.

Every time you speak, you should have a micro-win to offer your audience. Something free. Something helpful. Something that moves them toward you. A checklist. A guide. A training. Whatever fits.

Lead magnets turn applause into action.

They're how you take someone who's inspired and give them a next step. They're your breadcrumb trail and they matter.

I have even created a guide called *31 Yummy Lead Magnets* to help you brainstorm irresistible ideas that tie into your offers.

Finally, if you feel overwhelmed, pause and breathe.

I know it's a lot of moving parts: bios, branding, talk titles, follow-up sequences. That's why I created my eleven-step checklist for speaker success. It helps you catch the things most people don't even *know* to prepare for.

You don't have to figure this out alone.

Whether you're just getting started or have been speaking for a while, but you're ready to scale, I'm your Julia Child. I've got the apron. I've got the ingredients. I know what burns and what blooms. I know the recipe inside out and will make sure that you do not miss a single ingredient.

I am ready to help you heat things up.

So let me ask you:

What's your favorite meal?

Maybe it's rich and cheesy. Maybe it's warm and comforting. Maybe it's spicy and bold.

But I bet it didn't happen by accident.

Great meals, like great talks, are built with intention.

And you? You've got something delicious to share.

Let's Get Cooking by Speaking!

DANNELLA BURNETT

As seen in Entrepreneur.com Magazine, the L.A. Tribune, USA Today and in her Best Selling Books: VISIBILITY Volumes 1-3, C.O.A.C.H., and In the Spotlight, as well as seen on hundreds of stages around the world, Dannella Burnett has grown her own 7-figure business through speaking and events Through her connections, millions of dollars have been generated and tens of thousands of lives impacted!

Dannella and her team help busy entrepreneurs host profitable and impactful events and get speakers on stages! She believes in multiple streams of income, collaboration, and always finding the win-win-win combination!

Dannella is the Owner of Encore Elite Events, Speakers Need To Speak, ICONMAKER, and Podcast Magazine. She is a creative force with a passion for connecting experts to those they serve through speaking & events while generating profitable and impactful visibility!

www.Facebook.com/groups/SpeakerGigs

ROUND PEG, REAL PROGRESS: HOW TO SUCCEED WITHOUT FORCING YOURSELF INTO SOMEONE ELSE'S BOX

Carolyn Cahn, RN, MHSA, NLP-TT, CCHT, IEMT

I tried.

But school didn't click. The way teachers talked, the way lessons were taught—it all felt like someone was broadcasting on a frequency I couldn't quite tune into. Nobody ever stopped to say, "Hey, maybe you learn differently." So instead, I just quietly absorbed the message: Something must be wrong with me.

Spoiler alert: It wasn't.

Not even a little.

It wasn't until my forties that I got diagnosed with ADHD. Forty-something years of doing mental gymnastics to stay afloat in a world that made no room for how my brain worked. And the moment I got the diagnosis, I didn't feel broken. I felt seen.

It explained so much, like how I could remember the plot of every movie I'd ever watched but somehow lose my phone while holding it. Or how studying felt like trying to read a textbook in the middle of a squirrel rave. There was nothing "wrong" with me!

Let me rewind.

I grew up above a deli in New York—literally. My parents owned a delicatessen, and our apartment was upstairs. Dad worked seven days a week, slicing cold cuts while making eggs, and yelling up the stairs to tell us breakfast was ready. Mom, bless her, wasn't so much into feeding children—she had the birds, the fish, the dog, and the cat covered, but the kids? Not so much.

It was chaotic. Loud. Messy. But in some weird way, it was also cozy. That was my foundation: high-volume survival, unsupervised independence, and a whole lot of cold cuts.

I put myself through school. Started nursing school. And failed out. Bad grades. No safety net. Just a big fat "You're not cut out for this." But I wouldn't let that be the end. A spark caught fire. And I decided—no, I'm going to do this.

So I did.

I clawed my way back. Earned first my two-year and then my four-year degree, then my master's. I moved to California, started studying hypnosis and neurolinguistic programming. Because somewhere, deep down, I knew I wanted to help people in a way that went far beyond charts and stethoscopes.

Eventually, I was recruited into the U.S. Public Health Service and stationed in San Francisco. I loved it. Made an impact. When I transferred to San Francisco, I also started working in correctional healthcare because I *liked* it. Twenty-five years in that setting, and it brought out the best in me.

In 2021, everything changed. An inmate punched me in the face. Broken bones, broken teeth, left me with a concussion and a two-year recovery.

PTSD. Pain. A massive life shift. But also?

Growth.

I didn't shrink. I stayed connected to something bigger than my pain. I got a service dog named Belle, who became one of the greatest gifts of my life. I moved back east to be near my people. And I started building a business—one that lets me show up for others in the ways I needed someone to show up for me.

Because here's the truth no one ever told me: Not everyone learns the same way. Not everyone thrives under the "just be more disciplined" model. Sometimes the magic starts when you finally understand how *you* work. And someone—anyone—believes that you can.

That's why I do this.

Because I know what it's like to have a dream and feel like you're the only one who doesn't know how to reach it.

You're not alone. And you're not broken. You just haven't been handed the right tools.

Let's change that.

Let's dig into the real stuff.

Have you ever been halfway down a path and suddenly realized it was never meant for you in the first place? Like waking up halfway to dental school and thinking, "Hold on. I hate plaque."

That's what life feels like without clarity. We start chasing degrees or jobs or relationships because someone said it was smart or responsible or would look good on Instagram. But if we never pause to ask ourselves what *we* want, we wake up one day with a resume full of achievements and a heart full of "meh."

Clarity starts with self-discovery—not the incense-burning, full-moon-journaling kind. I'm talking about the real, raw kind of self-discovery. The kind where you ask yourself questions that matter. What makes you belly laugh? What makes you cry ugly? What makes you jump out of bed without even checking your phone?

What's your *why*?

Why this job? Why this relationship? Why this city where it snows in April and your neighbors don't shovel?

Why do you feel stuck?

Why did you give up on your dream of becoming a tap-dancing veterinarian?

These questions aren't just for entertainment. They're a GPS reroute to your own inner wisdom. And trust me, it leads somewhere better than where you've been headed.

But getting that clarity? It requires clearing out the mental closet. The one full of false beliefs about what you're supposed to be. Yes, it's uncomfortable. Yes, stuff will fall on your head. But once you make room, you'll start seeing yourself clearly. The glorious, awkward, powerful you.

And from that place, you can finally move forward.

Not just toward something.

But toward something that *feels like yours*.

Now, once you've got clarity, here's where it gets juicy: uncovering the root cause of what's keeping you stuck.

Let me ask you something. Have you ever picked up your phone to check the time... and then found yourself twenty minutes deep into a video of a raccoon riding a bicycle while eating cotton candy?

Yeah. Me, too.

We live in a world where distraction is practically an Olympic sport. But if we're being honest, a lot of our "bad habits" aren't really about laziness or lack of willpower. They're symptoms. Signals. Red flags from the deeper parts of us, waving wildly and yelling, "Hey! Something's not working!"

The scrolling. The snacking. The obsessing over tracking a package we ordered five minutes ago—it's not about the thing itself. It's about what that thing is *trying* to do for us. Distract us. Soothe us. Protect us from something we don't want to face.

I had a client once who told me she was addicted to texting. "I have to be available for everyone, all the time," she said. I looked at her and said, "You know they make airplane mode for that, right?"

When we dig underneath our habits—past the judgment and the shame—we find needs that are totally valid. And once we identify the *real* need? We can meet it in a healthier, more aligned way.

That's where the magic happens.

Now let's talk goals. Because once you know what's driving you and what's been holding you back, it's time to move forward. In a focused, intentional, "yes I made a plan and yes I actually followed it" kind of way.

Seriously—goal setting isn't just about checking boxes. It's about creating a roadmap your brain can follow. Otherwise, you're just driving in circles around the same emotional cul-de-sac, wondering why you're dizzy and drained.

This is where SMARTER goals come in. Specific. Measurable. Achievable. Relevant. Time-bound. Ecological. Reevaluate. It sounds like something from a corporate retreat. But I promise, it works. When you turn a vague wish like "I want to be successful" into something clear—like "I want to write three chapters of my book in the next 30 days"—you give your brain a win it can actually reach for.

And when you get that win? Your brain throws a little dopamine dance party. And suddenly you're not someone who "tries." You're someone who *follows through*.

Now let's bring in the grown-up stuff. Time management and prioritization.

I once made a to-do list that said:

1. Wake up
2. Be amazing
3. Conquer the world

Then I hit snooze five times and lost the list.

Time management isn't about being perfect. It's about being realistic. Learning to focus on one thing at a time. Learning how to set priorities and *stick to them*. Not just color-coding your calendar so it *looks* productive while you accomplish absolutely nothing.

When you learn how to plan your time with intention, you stop surviving your day and start *owning* it. You become the person who says, "Done," not "I'll get to it later." You breathe. You execute. You succeed.

Success doesn't come from doing *more*. It comes from doing *what matters*—with a plan.

And while we're at it—can we talk about relationships?

I used to think "networking" meant pretending to love mini quiches while standing awkwardly in a hotel ballroom with a plastic name tag on my chest. Turns out, it's just code for "making friends on purpose."

Relationship building is one of the most underrated success strategies out there. It's the bridge between where you are and where you want to go. And no, I'm not just talking about schmoozing at conferences. I'm talking about building real connections. People who support you, cheer for you, and text you back when you're having a meltdown in Target.

Don't underestimate the power of relationship building. Success isn't a solo sport. And sometimes, the best strategy starts with simply asking, "Want to grab coffee?"

Especially for those of us with ADHD or nontraditional brains, connection matters. Because the world is full of expectations that don't fit us. And if we try to do it alone, it's easy to feel like we're failing.

If you've ever felt like you're one productivity hack away from having your life together... and that hack *never* seems to work for you?

I want you to hear this loud and clear:
It was never you.

It was the box you were told you had to fit into.

Some of us aren't box people. We're round pegs. Emotional tornados. Sideways thinkers with brilliant ideas and messy desks. And that's okay..

I didn't have that when I was growing up. No guidance counselor ever sat me down and said, "Carolyn, here's how your brain works. Let's build a plan that fits." I had to figure it out the hard way. But now? I've built something different.

It's not a shiny checklist. It's not a one-size-fits-all program. It's a personal process that helps *you* uncover how *you* learn, move, thrive, and succeed.

And if you've been waiting for permission?

This is it..

What you need... is what Venus Williams said:
"You have to believe in yourself when no one else does—that makes you a winner right there."

So believe in yourself.

Even if your inner critic sounds like a karaoke singer who won't give up the mic.

Even if your dream is still in sweatpants, scrolling aimlessly, and waiting for a reason to show up.

Because I'm here to tell you: Any bad habit can become a benefit.

With the right perspective.

And the right problem-solving.

Let's figure it out—together.

You're not behind. You're just beginning.

And that dream of yours?

It's time to get it dressed and out the door.

CAROLYN CAHN

Carolyn Cahn is a seasoned Success Coach and Registered Nurse with over 35 years of experience in empowering adults to transform their lives. With degrees from George Washington University and Alfred University, along with certifications in NLP, Coaching, Hypnosis, Medical Hypnosis and Stage Hypnosis and IEMT, Carolyn combines a wealth of knowledge with practical expertise.

Specializing in guiding individuals who are burned out or seeking change, she helps clients release negative experiences and achieve their personal and professional goals. Carolyn assists clients in overcoming emotional hurdles linked to challenging memories.

Caroyn is a bestselling author whose impressive career includes managing 18 clinics and collaborating with various companies to foster healthier employees in the workplaces. She is dedicated to helping individuals harness their strengths to tackle challenges such as low self-esteem, ADHD, and burnout, leading them to a more fulfilling life.

www.CarolynCahn.com

MESSAGE OVER MADNESS: HOW TO DITCH CONFUSION AND CREATE MARKETING THAT CONVERTS

Alexis Caldicott

Cheat on your girlfriend. Not your workout.

That's not the kind of advice you expect to see splashed across a national ad campaign, right?

And yet—that's exactly what Reebok thought would sell sneakers.

Yes, *that* Reebok, the multibillion-dollar sportswear giant. Someone somewhere in a very expensive office said, "Let's run with that." And they did—right into a full-blown PR disaster. Within hours of global backlash, they yanked the ad and issued the corporate version of, "Oops, our bad. We don't advocate cheating … in *any* form."

How many marketing execs lost their jobs that day?

But wait—it gets better.

Some other iconic fails? Pepsi once thought it would be a great idea to cast Kendall Jenner as a peacemaker between protestors and police during a tense social justice demonstration. Her weapon of choice? A can of soda. I'm not kidding. Apparently, a Pepsi is all it takes to solve systemic oppression. That campaign was so tone-deaf, it actually made history—and not the good kind. The president of PepsiCo's marketing division stepped down six months later.

Still not done.

Audi, in what can only be described as an epic lapse in judgment, ran a commercial where the groom's *mother* inspects the bride at the altar like a used car. Lip pinch, ear tug, teeth check. And the slogan? "An important decision must be made carefully." You'd think *someone* in the room would've said, "This feels a little too much like objectification meets auto showroom…" But no. Another day, another messaging fail.

Now, while I'm clearly having some fun here—these aren't just juicy stories I tell over cocktails. They illustrate a deeper truth: **Messaging has the power to move people.**

The question is—will your message move people to *buy*? Or to *back away slowly while writing a snarky tweet*?

That's what I help businesses figure out. I help them get clear, consistent, and strategic with messaging and marketing that eliminate the competition. Not blend in. Not barely survive. **Eliminate.**

But here's what stings: Right now, a lot of business owners are out there just farting in the wind.

Yes, I said it.

You're putting stuff out there—LinkedIn posts, reels, email blasts, webinars—and none of it's landing. Or if it is, it's not converting. Not filling your pipeline. Not turning into cash in the bank. You're exhausted, overwhelmed, and wondering why none of this seems to work the way you were promised it would in that $27 course you bought from the TikTok coach with the ring light and a whiteboard.

You're chasing visibility like it's the goal—but visibility without clarity is just noise. It's spaghetti on the wall. And the wall? It's already covered in everyone else's spaghetti.

You're following trends from random internet strangers, DMing cold leads, questioning if you should start a YouTube channel or launch a summit. Meanwhile, you don't even have a core message that connects.

No wonder your competition is eating your lunch.

You've got brilliant offers and a heart of gold—but you're confusing the people you're trying to serve. And you know what they say: Confused minds don't buy. But I'll take it a step further—*confused entrepreneurs* don't sell either.

Your business isn't broken. Your dream isn't too big. You're not too early, too late, or too anything.

You're unclear.

And clarity? That's fixable.

You didn't start your business to become a full-time marketer. You started because you wanted to make money, make a difference, maybe change some lives. But somewhere along the way, the marketing monster started eating up all your time, confidence, and voice.

That's where I come in. I help people find the *through line*—that core message that threads through everything: your emails, your bios, your talks, your funnels, your "Hey, what do you do?" answer at the bar. Because when that message clicks? Everything clicks.

And I've seen what happens when it does. Clients making $50K from one email. $40K from a webinar. $13K in her very first month of business—without even having an offer before we started. I've seen what happens when the noise gets stripped away and the message gets turned all the way up.

My own business did half a million last year. I did $250K in three days. Not from luck. Not from hustle culture. From clarity. From **message.**

And just to be clear, I don't care what business you're in. Insurance. Coaching. Wigs. (Yes, wigs. The Wig Lady made $50K from one email.) It doesn't matter what you sell. It matters **what you say.**

Now if you're wondering how the opera-singing, Juilliard-dodging, music-obsessed woman became a messaging strategist, here's the quick remix:

I started in music. Viola. Opera. Third-grade prodigy vibes. Juilliard came calling. My mom said no. Broadway offered an understudy slot. Again, Mom said no. (Thanks, Mom.) So I kept playing, kept singing, and eventually became a classically trained opera singer. Then a music therapist. Then a business coach. Then an event strategist.

Somewhere along the way, people started asking me: "How are you filling these rooms? How are you getting clients to pay attention? How are you doing this?"

Spoiler: It wasn't the venue. It was the *copy*. The message. The words that turned browsers into buyers.

I realized my real magic wasn't logistics. It was pulling someone's brilliance out of their head, organizing it into something powerful, and turning that into messaging that actually sells.

So I hung up the viola, and I stepped into the thing I do best.

Now let's talk about how this works—how messaging and marketing can shift everything—for your business and your life.

If your business were a house, messaging would be the foundation. I know, I know—most people want to jump straight to picking out the gold hardware and the marble countertops. But if the foundation's cracked? That dream kitchen is going to collapse into the dirt.

Messaging is the soul of your business. It's not a cute tagline. It's not a clever caption. It's the reason someone chooses you instead of scrolling right past. It's how you show people what you stand for, what you solve, and why it matters to them. Without a solid message, all your marketing is just... wall art in a house built on sand.

Now, you *can* build with anything. Funnels. Podcasts. Speaking gigs. Instagram reels with you pointing at text bubbles like a mime in a crop top. Doesn't matter. Those are materials. What matters is the base.

And when the base is strong? The rest becomes simple, not stressful.

But building that message starts with clarity. Real, unfiltered clarity about what you do, who it's for, and why it matters. That's why I use five core messaging questions that are the holy grail of clarity. I like to call them the "Dragon Slayer Questions." Because, yes—this is your hero's journey.

1. **What's the problem you solve?**

   This is your dragon. It's not a baby problem. It's not a mild inconvenience. It's the thing that's burning down villages and keeping your people up at night. Get specific. Get real. Don't sugarcoat the smoke.

2. **Who do you solve it for?**

   These are your villagers. Not *all* the villagers—*your* villagers. The ones you're meant to serve. The ones who feel seen when you speak. If your message tries to speak to everyone, it lands with no one.

3. How do you solve it?

This is your sword. Your special sauce. Your framework, your method, your unique twist on solving the dragon problem. Don't just list features—show how your *approach* is different.

4. 4. What is the solution you provide?

Here's where you get clear on the actual offer. What are you giving them? What's the container? Is it a program, a product, a session, a wig (hey, Wig Lady!)—whatever it is, be specific.

5. 5. What does that solution allow them to do/be/have?

This is the real magic. The transformation. What does life look like after the dragon's gone? More time? More money? Peace of mind? A business that doesn't feel like a panic attack in heels?

Answer those five questions with honesty and specificity, and you'll never be confused about how to market again.

Now, let's talk momentum—because once your message is clear, you've got to get it out there. And not with cringey, cold-pitch DMs or bro-marketing nonsense. That stuff doesn't work anymore—if it ever did.

You've got to market in a way that feels good, lands right, and builds trust.

That's why I'm obsessed with **education-based marketing**. It's not about pushing. It's about guiding. Think of your audience like toddlers at a birthday party. You can't just hand them a plate of steamed broccoli and expect applause. You've got to start with the cake.

The cake is the thing they think they want: "How do I get more leads?" "How do I get unstuck?" "How do I make sales without feeling gross?"

You give them cake.

But inside the cake? Nutrients. Real talk. Strategy. The stuff they actually *need* to grow.

"Let them eat cake," said Marie Antoinette. Same energy—but make it strategic.

This is how you earn trust. You give value up front. You teach something meaningful. You meet them where they are, and then walk them where they need to go. I call it the **Itty Bitty Carb Crumb Treatment**—you breadcrumb people to your offer, one delicious insight at a time.

That's what the **PS Model** is all about—Problem ▢ Solution. But not in a "Here's your problem, now buy my thing" kind of way. It's a story. A journey. You show them the dragon. You walk with them. You make them care. And when you finally present the solution, it feels obvious. Inevitable. Like destiny with a payment plan.

One client of mine used this model and went from crickets to a sold-out program. Nothing changed in her offer. We just changed how we talked about it. We led with cake. We sprinkled in crumbs. And when we finally served the full meal? Her audience was *hungry*.

This is what it looks like to lead with message. You don't chase. You don't beg. You guide. You show. You serve.

And that brings me to what I really want to say to you as we wrap this up.

Because this isn't just about selling things or growing your email list. It's about being seen. Heard. Paid. Trusted.

Marketing stops being a chore. Clients stop ghosting. You stop whispering what you do and start declaring it—clearly, powerfully, with a voice that makes people *stop scrolling and pay attention.*

You weren't born to be ignored. You weren't born to blend in.

You were born to stand out. To lead. To light it up with clarity so strong, it eliminates the competition before they even open their mouths.

And if you're ready for that? I'm your girl.

Let's fix your message. Let's stop farting in the wind. Let's bake some nutrient-filled cake and serve it to the people who need you most.

Because you were not born to be silent. You were born to make noise.

ALEXIS CALDICOTT

Alexis Caldicott is an International Speaker, Messaging & Marketing Consultant that has taught thousands of business owners around the world how to strategically use their message & talents to get more clients & make a bigger impact.

Known as the "Queen of Education Based Marketing", Alexis' blend of psychology, sales copywriting, & education-based marketing has helped her clients gross millions of dollars in sales.

She has been featured on NBC, Fox News, CBS, and Boston Herald, graduated on the Dean's List with Honors in psychology, and (fun fact) is a classically trained opera singer.

www.AlexisCaldicott.com

THE POWER BENEATH THE LAYERS: UNPEELING THE TRUTH YOU'VE ALWAYS CARRIED WITHIN

Genine R. Carter

You probably didn't expect to be compared to a cabbage today. But trust me—it's more accurate than you think.

If you've ever cut open a cabbage and really looked inside, you know what I mean. It's not just a vegetable. It's a swirling, layered roadmap—tight spirals wrapped around deeper folds, all leading toward a center most people never see.

And that? That's you.

You started out whole. And then life happened. Layer after layer—experiences, heartbreaks, wins, fears, awkward school dances, jobs you stayed too long at, people who didn't see you—all of it wrapped around the core of who you are.

Most of us never slow down long enough to examine it. We just keep going, feeling like something's missing but unsure what or why. That feeling? That's what I call mystery cabbage energy.

The part of you sitting silently in the back of the fridge, wrapped up tight, pretending to be fine but slowly growing stale. Because no one's taken the time to slice it open and really see what's going on inside.

But when you *do*—when you begin to explore the layers, honor them, understand them—something incredible happens. You stop searching for your worth in other people's eyes. You stop molding yourself into a version of "acceptable." You start showing up as *you.*

Fully. Boldly. Lovingly.

This is the moment in your life where everything shifts.

Because once you know your own layers, you stop needing to be fixed. You stop needing to be understood. You start loving what's been there all along.

That's the price of real freedom: self-love.

And not the glittery kind that looks good on Instagram. I'm talking about the gritty, raw, honest self-love that sits with your mess and says, "You're worthy anyway."

I'm talking about the kind of love that creates real change.

Because when you love yourself like that, you stop chasing relationships that drain you. You stop settling for jobs that don't see your brilliance. You stop feeling numb in moments that are supposed to feel joyful.

You begin to live. Fully live your life.

This is the heart of my work.

I help people heal—not just cope, but *release.* I use emotion mapping, sound healing, energy work, spiritual coaching, and deep intuitive tools such as the Akashic records that help you find the exact moment your patterns were born.

Because they all started somewhere.

Maybe you constantly over give in relationships. Maybe you can't hold onto money. Maybe your default setting is anxiety no matter how well things are going. That didn't come out of nowhere. There's a root. And I help you find it.

Emotion mapping is like inner detective work. We trace the emotion to its origin. We uncover the moment—sometimes years ago, sometimes seemingly small—that planted a belief deep inside you. And even though it might seem random, your subconscious locked it in and started building a life around it.

But once we bring that belief into the light?

You can finally let it go. Forever.

And that's when the real healing begins.

But healing isn't just looking backward. It's learning how to be in your body and your life now. And let's start with the basics: how you treat yourself.

You plug your phone in before the battery dies. You buy it a case. You protect it from damage. But you? You'll run on 1% energy for weeks, convince yourself you're fine, and feel guilty for taking a nap.

We've been taught that burnout is noble. That self-sacrifice is strength. That rest is laziness. And it's all wrong.

Self-love means honoring your energy like it matters—because it *does.* You are not a machine. You are a living, breathing source of light, and you deserve to be treated accordingly.

That means learning the language of your many selves.

Because you're not just one person. You are your ego. Your emotional body. Your mental body. Your inner child. Your shadow. And they all have different needs, triggers, voices, fears.

Ever overreacted to something "small" and wondered why you felt so overwhelmed? That wasn't your logic talking. That was your inner child remembering a moment when they didn't feel safe. Or your shadow resisting vulnerability. Or your ego trying to protect you the only way it knows how.

When you learn to recognize which version of you is speaking, you shift out of chaos and into awareness.

And from there, you can build something sacred: self-boundaries.

Not just the kind you set with others, but the ones you uphold within yourself. Self-boundaries say: I don't abandon myself just to make others comfortable. I don't override my intuition to avoid disappointing someone. I don't hustle for worthiness—I already am.

And here's the beautiful truth: boundaries don't require explanation when you're living in alignment. People *feel* them. You walk differently. You speak differently. You hold your space with a kind of quiet authority that says, "This is who I am. And I don't shrink."

But none of that works without self-vulnerability.

You can't protect what you won't admit exists.

That means telling yourself the truth. Sitting with your emotions instead of numbing them. Being honest about what hurts, even when it's messy. That's not weakness. That's power.

Self-vulnerability creates self-trust. And self-trust becomes the foundation of everything else.

Because when you trust yourself, you don't need constant reassurance. You don't beg life to be easier. You rise to meet what comes.

That's how you move from reaction to creation.

And when you combine all of this—awareness, boundaries, vulnerability, healing—you start to feel something you haven't felt in a long time: energy.

Your life force. Your prana.

You stop running on fumes. You stop dragging yourself through the day. You start waking up with clarity. With strength. With purpose.

Because when your energy is flowing freely, you're not just surviving—you're thriving.

You feel connected. To yourself. To others. To something bigger.

And in that space, something sacred returns: joy. Pure unadulterated joy.

Not the performative, look-at-me kind. The quiet, steady, soul-deep kind. The kind that doesn't need a reason. The kind that just *is*.

That's what happens when you come back home to yourself.

When you stop trying to earn love and start becoming it.

When you stop waiting for permission and start choosing freedom.

That's the invitation I'm holding open for you.

Because I know what it's like to feel lost. I know what it's like to be told you're too much. I know what it's like to carry the weight of an entire family and still feel invisible.

But I also know what it's like to break free.

To finally meet yourself—fully, honestly, unapologetically—and say, "There you are. I've been waiting for you."

You don't need to start over.

You just need to come home.

So take a breath. Maybe more.

Then look inward.

And say it with your whole, glorious, layered self:

I am cabbage. And I am free.

GENINE R. CARTER

Meet Genine Carter—intuitive healer, energy medicine practitioner, and host of Heal Out Loud Podcast. Her work blends Sound Healing, Spiritual Coaching, Guided Meditation, and Emotion Mapping to help others release trauma and embrace wholeness. Genine's healing journey began with the ancient practice of Chi gong (or Qigong). She later began to explore the Akashic Records and other transformative practices. Now, she's on a mission to guide others toward alignment, self-love, and empowered living. Tune into Heal Out Loud Podcast (on all major platforms) for real conversations that inspire growth, activate your spirit, and remind you—you're not alone on this path.

www.Linktr.ee/GeninesHealingClinic

UNFORGETTABLE: THE STORY ONLY YOU CAN TELL

Yvonne Chotzen

Hollywood Producer | Federal Litigator | Storytelling Strategist

> *"Tell the story that costs you something to share—because that's the one that changes everything."*

Last year, over 825 million movie tickets were sold in the U.S. and Canada. Nearly **$9 billion** in box office revenue. And that's just the movies. Add in five hundred-plus TV shows, and you're looking at **$225 billion** in revenue, over 5.4 billion viewers, consumption rising year after year, and a world utterly consumed by one thing:

Story.

Not a brand strategy. Not a sales funnel. Not a marketing message.

Just a story.

Because story is the one thing that cuts through the noise of our too-loud, too-busy, too-scrollable world.

Story is what captivates. What connects. What converts.

Story is what makes us feel something. And in a world addicted to attention, if you can't make someone feel something ... you disappear.

But here's what I've learned—what I've lived—on both sides of the courtroom and the camera:

We just don't need *more* stories.

We need **deeper** stories.

Because most of the stories we're telling? They skim the surface. They impress. They sell.

But they don't connect.

Not soul to soul.

Not heart to heart.

The Story that Stopped Hollywood

Years ago, I was in federal court in downtown Los Angeles, representing a client whose case had been all over the Honolulu headlines—a brutal murder, a missing child, a woman fleeing across seven states.

As I rose to speak before the judge, I noticed something strange. People were flooding into the courtroom. I leaned across to the prosecutor and whispered, "What's going on?"

He nodded toward my client.

"They're Hollywood producers," he said. "They want her life rights."

Of course they did. Her story had everything: a love triangle, a military murder, a kidnapped daughter, a manipulative grandmother. The stakes were massive—and real.

I asked the judge for a recess and ran down to the lockup.

Kathy—my client—was sitting in a holding cell with nothing but a red apple and a napkin.

I leaned in. "The courtroom is full of producers. They want your story."

She didn't even blink. She grabbed the pen from my hand, wrote on the napkin, and slid it back.

Yvonne Chotzen is my producer.

Then she looked me dead in the eye and said, "Get lots of money for my baby, you hear?"

She meant her daughter—the one she'd lost custody of, the one she was trying to protect.

Three days later, I was pitching the story to NBC.

It became a four-hour miniseries starring Martin Sheen and Patty Duke—the highest-rated miniseries in eight years.[*]

And my phone hasn't stopped buzzing since.

(And yes … I auditioned to play myself. Didn't get it. Turns out, I wasn't destined to be an actress.)

But I *was* destined to be a storyteller.

From Bedtime to Boardroom

I've been telling stories my whole life.

As the eldest of eight, I inherited bedtime story duty from my dad. I spun tales every night to lull my siblings to sleep—and watched how the right words could light up their eyes.

Later, I started a birthday party puppet show company telling stories from a decorated box with my younger siblings—we were booked every weekend.

---

[*] **A Matter of Justice** mini series for television, starring Martin Sheen and Patty Duke

My stage just kept getting bigger.

I became a columnist. A CEO. A federal trial lawyer. A Hollywood producer. A storytelling strategist for top performers and powerful teams.

But in every room—from courtroom to C-suite to live stage—I've seen one truth over and over:

The most powerful story you can tell ... is the one that costs you something.

When a Story Isn't Polished—But True

Let me be blunt: We're drowning in stories.

Reels. Posts. Podcasts. Speeches. Scroll your feed for five minutes and you'll see a hundred origin stories and rags-to-riches transformations. Everyone's sharing.

But few are connecting.

Because we've turned stories into performances, into perfectly branded TED Talks, into "Let me tell you about my journey" humblebrags.

Here's the truth:

The stories that move people... are not the ones that make you look good.

They're the ones that make you feel **seen**.

And being seen is scary. Because those stories—the real ones—are still tender. Still raw. Still alive in your body.

They're the moments you've never fully told.

One client found hers:

"I'm ten years old. The belt is coming down. Again. I step between it and my mom and say: "Stop.""

It was the moment she first used her voice and stood up for someone she loved. Her life calling was inside that story. Today, she coaches people to leave abusive relationships.

Or the NICU nurse holding a premature baby who had just died and had to tell a mother that her baby didn't make it. Today, she runs a program that supports frontline healthcare workers in trauma healing.

Those aren't "content."

They're truth. And that truth? That's where the heart of your story lives.

Why It Works: The Brain Doesn't Lie

This isn't just poetic. It's neuroscience.

According to studies in *Harvard Business Review*, emotionally resonant stories light up more regions of the brain than facts ever could—especially those responsible for empathy and human connection.

Your audience isn't just *hearing* your story.

They're feeling it as if it is happening to them.

And that's when the magic happens: Brain scans show the listener's brain literally starts to sync with the speaker's.

We call it *neural coupling*.
No wonder stories heal teams, connect strangers, and build trust.
It's biological.

So how do you tell a story that anchors at this level?

The Three D's of Storytelling Mastery

Whether you're a CEO, coach, creative, or keynote speaker—this is the roadmap I've used with hundreds of clients to unlock unforgettable stories.

1. Discover

Find the story *beneath* the story. The one that reveals your values, your why, and your transformation. Not the highlight reel—the heartbeat.

Ask inciting questions like:

- What moment changed everything?
- When did I first use my voice?
- What memory makes my chest tighten?

Then write for five minutes—no edits, no filter. And read it aloud.

Notice what line makes your voice catch?

That's the one.

2. Design

Now we shape it. And for that, we borrow from Hollywood.

Start in the middle of the conflict. Drop us *in* the moment.

Flat version: "I booked a flight and traveled to Italy with my husband..."

Hollywood version:

"There I was at St. Peter's Basilica in the Vatican, a fifty-one-year-old Jewish woman desperate to get pregnant, waiting for my Papal womb blessing."

(Yes. That really happened—healthy twins at fifty-five!)

Use rhythm. Contrast. Dialogue. Tension. Emotion. Make us *feel*.

3. Deliver

This is where you rise.

Whether you're on stage, in a boardroom, or on Zoom—show up.

Own your space. Use your voice. Let your gestures carry your message.

Don't aim to be perfect. Aim to be *present*.

That's what people remember.

This Isn't Just Storytelling—This Is Legacy

When I worked with a corporate team at Starbucks, they were competitive, disconnected, and bristling with tension. I didn't give them a leadership model.

I asked them to tell their stories.

One senior leader shared how, at eight, she walked in her best white shoes through the desert for miles when her dad was refused gas because of their ethnicity. Her colleagues had never heard that story.

Now they saw her. They felt her.

They never worked the same again.

Because story doesn't just change minds.

It changes hearts.

And that connection is where trust builds and healing happens.

So Let Me Ask You...

Are you ready to tell the story that only you can tell?
The one that opens doors you didn't even know were locked?

The story that moves the room. That unlocks your business. That brings your voice out of hiding.

Because someone out there is waiting for your story.

Waiting to feel seen. Waiting for a spark. Waiting for you to go first.

So don't wait for perfect. Don't wait for permission.

Just tell it.

And when you're ready to craft it, shape it, and share it like the world-changer you are—I'll be right here.

Helping you **tell stories like Hollywood.**

Helping you **get more attention by touching more hearts.**

Helping you **change the world—one unforgettable story at a time.**

YVONNE E. CHOTZEN

Yvonne Chotzen, award-winning Hollywood Producer and former trial attorney, helps entrepreneurs and professionals unleash Hollywood-style storytelling as a powerful business catalyst. Blending legal precision with cinematic impact, she ignites visibility, connection, and revenue. Trained in federal criminal trials, her 3-step storytelling method delivered courtroom wins—and later, Hollywood deals. One murder case became an NBC miniseries, launching her film career. With movies seen by millions, her standout, The Rosa Parks Story starring Angela Bassett, won the NAACP Image Award for Best Movie of the Year. Today, Yvonne empowers entrepreneurs to tell heartfelt stories that captivate audiences, elevate presence, ignite connection, and drive results using her proven "UNFORGETTABLE" Hollywood storytelling strategy.

www.YvonneChotzen.com

YOU'RE THE VISIONARY, NOT THE VA: HOW TO STOP DOING IT ALL AND STILL GROW BIG

Brandi Cox

"The link doesn't work."

Four little words. One massive emotional landslide.

You're in the middle of your Zoom workshop. The slides are sharp, the chat is buzzing, your delivery is on fire—you drop the offer link and BOOM. There it is: "The link doesn't work." Then another. And another.

You click it. It really doesn't work. Cue internal screaming.

And suddenly, digital doom hijacks your perfect, polished, heart-pouring moment. Your pulse spikes. Your mouth goes dry. You're clicking your own link while trying to keep your face from melting off in front of eighty-seven potential clients. You wanted this to be your turning point. Instead, your tech is tap-dancing on your last nerve.

I know that moment. I *live* in that moment—because that's when you call me.

I'm Brandi. Tech whisperer. Automation architect. Systems surgeon. Disabled combat veteran with an autistic brain obsessed with solving puzzles. I see the chaos you're drowning in—and I organize it so your business can breathe again.

Most entrepreneurs try to duct tape their backend together with Google searches, caffeine, and Canva PDFs. They're running seven different platforms with three different logins, and still wondering why nothing talks to anything else.

Sound familiar?

It's not your fault. You didn't start your business because you love tech. You started it because you wanted to help people. To change lives. To serve.

But now, instead of being the visionary, you've become the IT department.

Let me say this clearly: **Profitable businesses outsource their technology and automation.** Not because they're lazy—but because they're smart. They know their energy is better spent changing lives, not changing passwords.

I build systems that do the heavy lifting for you. Email automations. Booking flows. Client onboarding. Funnels. CRMs that don't make you cry. Because tech should support your genius, not sabotage it.

And yes, I've been where you are. I built this business from a bed—while managing chronic pain, depression, and a body that said, "We're done." I automated everything. Then I delegated. Then I gamified it. Because if I'm going to show up, it better be fun.

Now I help people like you do the same.

And I do it with a little inspiration from *Doctor Who*.

If you've never watched it, don't worry. It's a British sci-fi show in which a brilliant, quirky hero travels through time with a trusty sonic screwdriver and a rotating cast of companions—solving problems, fixing timelines, saving the day.

It's basically entrepreneurship.

You're the hero. Your business is your time machine. And you need three things to fly it without crashing into a black hole: a sonic screwdriver (automation), a team of companions (delegation), and a TARDIS manual (processes).

Let's break them down.

First up: Automation—Your Sonic Screwdriver

Automation is the system that takes repetitive tasks off your plate and makes them happen behind the scenes without you lifting a finger. Think: welcome emails, appointment confirmations, abandoned cart reminders, invoicing, follow-ups—the stuff that has to happen, but doesn't require your magic touch.

Before one of my clients automated, she was stuck in the land of sticky notes and browser tabs—sending contracts manually, chasing down missed calls, waking up in a cold sweat, wondering if she'd remembered to invoice that one client from three weeks ago.

We cleaned up her funnel. We set triggers, tags, and time delays. Now? She wakes up to paid invoices, booked calls, and—wait for it—*free time*. Real free time. The kind you don't have to earn with exhaustion.

Automation gives you your hours back. Your sanity. Your Saturday afternoons. And the best part? Once it's set up, it keeps working—while you nap, while you speak, while you eat tacos and binge-watch something with dragons.

It is the most powerful, underused force in most businesses.

And if it sounds scary or confusing, or like something you'd rather eat nails than figure out, that's okay. I make it feel like magic. You tell me what you want to happen—I build the invisible engine that makes it happen.

Next: Delegation Strategy—Your Companion Team

You were never meant to do this alone.

I don't care how brilliant, capable, or scrappy you are—running a business without support is like trying to fly the TARDIS solo on your first day. You're gonna crash into a volcano.

Delegation strategy isn't just about hiring people. It's about knowing what to *stop* doing. What to get off your plate. What to hand over to someone who won't procrastinate on it, hate it, or set it on fire by accident.

One client of mine was manually uploading every client contact into her CRM ... *from her phone*. Her actual, tiny-screened phone. She said she didn't have time to train someone. I said, "Girl, you don't have time *not* to."

We brought in a VA for ten hours a week. Suddenly, she had space to breathe. She remembered what weekends felt like. She messaged me with three words: "I feel human."

Delegation isn't a weakness. It's a weapon.

Your first hire might be a virtual assistant. Or a tech implementer. Or someone to just log into your email and tell you which messages are worth reading.

You don't need a big team. You need the *right* support, targeted where it matters most. And a strategy to help you stop micromanaging and start leading.

Finally: Processes—Your TARDIS Manual

I know, I know. "Processes" sounds like something you'd rather set on fire than sit down and document. But stick with me.

A process is just a clear, repeatable set of steps for anything you do more than once. Client onboarding? That's a process. Sending your weekly email? Process. Publishing a podcast episode? Yep, process.

Without them, you're just reinventing the wheel every week—and wondering why your wheels keep falling off.

Processes save you from your own future frustration. They let you hand off tasks without telepathy. They let your team step in when you're sick, traveling, or just not feeling it.

One of my clients had a killer podcast but no structure. Every week she'd panic, re-record things, forget to upload the show notes, and generally spiral. We built her a workflow—with templates, reminders, checklists—and suddenly she was publishing on time, stress-free, and getting more listeners than ever.

A process turns chaos into confidence.

It doesn't have to be fancy. It just has to live *somewhere other than your brain.*

Now, when I walk clients through these three tools—automation, delegation, and processes—they usually ask, "Brandi, is this really going to make *that* big a difference?"

So let me hit you with some math. Businesses that use their CRM (that's customer relationship management software, for the record) effectively can boost their conversion rates by over **300 percent**. That's not a typo. That's the difference between scraping by and scaling.

Every missed email. Every clunky onboarding experience. Every glitchy calendar link. It's not just annoying—it's leaking money, leaking energy, leaking *momentum*.

You were born to do something amazing. Something real. Something that changes lives. But if your tech systems aren't supporting that, you're doing double the work for half the results.

So let me give you your screwdriver.

Let me help you build your dream crew.

Let's write your manual together—so the business you've built can finally start working *for* you.

Allons-y.

Let's have a real moment, shall we?

Nobody—and I mean nobody—starts a business because they're dying to fiddle with calendar sync settings or obsess over why an automation didn't fire.

You didn't become a coach, healer, speaker, or creative because you dreamed of late nights battling with email automations. And not a single human on this planet has ever said, "You know what really lights me up? CRM integration."

You started your business because you had a calling.

You had a skill, a gift, a spark that refused to stay quiet. You wanted to help people. You wanted to create something meaningful. Maybe even change lives.

But now?

You're knee-deep in digital duct tape, stuck fixing things you were never meant to touch, and wondering why your business feels like a part-time IT job with a side of burnout.

Let me lovingly say this: You're not bad at tech. You're just doing too much of what's *not your job*.

And it's costing you more than time.

Every hour you spend DIY-ing your backend is an hour you're not coaching, creating, speaking, selling, leading.

And let's talk about cost for a second—because I see this math mistake all the time.

I'll ask a client, "What do you charge per hour?" She says, "$150."

Then I say, "Cool, and how many hours did you spend last week trying to figure out how to connect your webinar platform to your CRM?"

"Umm ... five?"

That's $750 of your genius down the drain.

Meanwhile, I've got systems, VAs, and automations that run for a fraction of that—and they don't take coffee breaks or cry over broken email templates.

You're not saving money by doing it all yourself.

It's robbing you of your momentum, your money, and your magic.

But here's the good news: It doesn't have to be this way.

You could be in Tahiti—umbrella drink in hand, toes in the sand—and your business could still be running. Emails are being sent. Payments are being processed. Clients are being onboarded. Notes are being synced. Appointments are being booked.

That's not a fantasy. That's what automation and delegation *give* you.

And that's what I help you build.

Not just a functioning business—but a business that's sustainable, scalable, and soul-aligned. One that doesn't crumble the moment you take a nap or step away. One that keeps humming along whether you're on stage or watching Netflix with your dog.

You're the architect.

You're the face.

So if you've been stuck in tech chaos, wondering if you can afford to get help—I lovingly say: You can't afford *not* to.

Let me come in with my snark, my spreadsheets, my mildly obsessive love for automations, and my full-body passion for building systems that *work*.

Let me fix the funnel so you can fuel your fire and automate the backend so you can lead from the front.

Because when you show up fully in your zone of genius, the whole world gets better.

And I'll be right behind you, wiring the machine, cheering you on, and whispering, "I got you" every step of the way.

If you remember one thing from this chapter—besides the fact that I literally snuggle with my phone like it's a security blanket— remember this:

You do what you do best. We'll do the rest.

Let's go build your freedom machine.

And let's have a hell of a good time doing it.

BRANDI COX

Brandi Cox is a combat veteran, gamer, and tech trail guide for entrepreneurs who are tired of doing everything alone. Through her company, Quest for Clients, she helps overwhelmed business owners ditch the chaos, automate the boring stuff, and build wildly profitable systems that actually work. Brandi believes profitable businesses outsource—and she's living proof you don't need to be loud or perfect to make big money doing what you love.

www.QuestForClients.com

DANCING LIKE A FOOL, SELLING LIKE A QUEEN: THE SLIGHTLY EMBARRASSING JOURNEY TO BECOMING A GREAT SPEAKER (AND FINALLY GETTING SEEN)

Alissa Crabtree, CEO and Speaker Coach

When I decided to try Zumba, I thought, "How hard could it be? I've been dancing at the club for years!"

But then the instructor walked in—this superhuman with tons of energy—and immediately launched into what felt like the choreography for Cirque du Soleil.

Within minutes, my arms were flailing in completely different directions from everyone else's.

While the class was gracefully salsa-stepping left, I stumbled to the right.

When they shimmied forward, I somehow ended up facing the back wall.

At one point, I got so tangled up that I nearly took out an entire row of innocent bystanders with my uncoordinated spin move.

The instructor kept shouting, "Now add some flavor! More hips! More passion!"

Meanwhile, I was just trying to figure out which foot went where without causing bodily harm.

By the end, I wasn't dancing, I was surviving.

I left the class looking like I'd been through a car wash without the car.

And you know what? That's exactly how I felt when I first started my business.

Overwhelmed. Disoriented. Desperately trying to follow a beat I couldn't hear.

Everyone had advice. "Post more on social media!" "Build a funnel!" "Start a podcast!"

So I did what many new entrepreneurs do. I tried everything. At once.

And like my wild Zumba moves, it wasn't working. I was exhausted, confused, and dangerously close to giving up.

But here's what I finally realized: Just like Zumba, business isn't about doing everything. It's about finding your rhythm and mastering one core move that gets you in sync before adding the fancy footwork.

That core move?

Speaking.

Not just talking. Not just showing up. But using your voice with the intention to be seen, heard, and remembered, because here's the truth: Only 9 percent of businesses make it to the 10-year mark.

Why?

Lack of profit. Declining revenue. Poor cash flow. Which all trace back to one fatal flaw: Not enough consistent leads.

And if you're not speaking, you're probably not selling.

But when you take the mic, everything shifts:

- **Authority Amplified:** You instantly position yourself as the expert in the room.
- **Connections Multiplied:** Speaking builds trust faster than any ad or funnel ever could.
- **Impact Expanded:** Your message lives beyond the moment, sparking momentum long after you leave the stage.

Let me tell you how I really learned the power of speaking.

When I started my first business as an education consultant, I was the ultimate hustler.

Every single morning, I called ten campuses. And every single time, I reached the same gatekeeper, the administrative assistant. If I was lucky, I got to leave a message. But most days? Just a polite, "No thank you," and a dial tone.

I emailed hundreds, if not thousands, of principals. Crickets.

I even drove across state lines, hand-delivering boxes of doughnuts and kolaches, just praying someone would talk to me.

Spoiler alert: The carbs didn't help. I still couldn't get past the front office.

It was defeating. It was exhausting. And worst of all, it wasn't working.

I remember my coach, Suzanne Evans, giving me a challenge: "Get eight no's a day."

Well, I was an overachiever. I could rack up those rejections like it was my job. (Unfortunately, it kind of was.)

A few clients trickled in through referrals, but they weren't enough to keep the business profitable. I was pouring in time, effort, energy, and my bank account was drying up faster than my will to cold-call another campus.

And then, an opportunity popped up: a principal conference three hours away. They were looking for exhibitors, and although I had never been one before, I was willing to try anything. It was a hefty investment, way outside my comfort zone, but it came with something different: a thirty-minute speaking slot.

I didn't know what I was doing. But I said yes.

I bought the booth. The fancy banner. I packed the swag table like a Pinterest board. I even busted out a few of my Zumba moves to get people to stop and talk.

And it worked... a little.

But when my moment to speak finally arrived?

That changed everything.

I stepped on stage, delivered a thirty-minute talk in the exhibit hall, and when I was done, principals lined up at my booth. I didn't have to chase them. I didn't have to beg for a meeting. They came to me.

By the end of that day, I had secured $80,000 in contracts from one speaking engagement! I was floored!

That, my friend, is the power of being seen and heard.

But here's the kicker: It wasn't just about being on stage. It was about knowing what to say and how to say it in a way that made people trust me with their problems and their budgets.

And that's exactly what we're diving into next. Because showing up with a mic in hand isn't enough. You need to know how to deliver.

Let's be honest. Speaking can feel just as intimidating as that first Zumba class.

You're afraid of messing up, of looking awkward, of being that person on stage who makes the room squirm.

And that's exactly why we need to talk about this. Because showing up unprepared isn't just a missed opportunity; it's a credibility killer.

So before you grab the mic and start salsa-ing your way into speaking, let's make sure you know what actually works.

Remember that first Zumba class I mentioned? Let's go back for a second.

Imagine if the instructor had kicked off the class by listing all his certifications and breaking down the history of Latin dance.

I would've walked out before the warm-up even started.

But instead, he blasted the music and pulled us straight into the energy. I didn't know what I was doing, but I paid attention.

Speaking is the same way.

If you want people to lean in, you've got to start strong. And I'm not talking about a polite "Hi, I'm so honored to be here" kind of strong.

I mean a grab-them-by-the-eyeballs, stop-them-in-their-tracks, "wait … what did she just say?" kind of strong.

So here is what you do:

- Do start with a hook, something bold, unexpected, or emotionally charged that grabs attention in the first thirty seconds.

Let me say that louder for the folks in the back: You don't have time to ease in. Your audience is deciding right now if they're going to lock in and listen … or mentally peace out and start planning what snack they're grabbing next.

This is the digital age. Attention spans are shorter than a TikTok trend. So make your opening count. Shock them. Make them laugh. Stir something up. Just don't waste it on pleasantries and a PowerPoint title slide. Because if they're not hooked early, they're gone. And if they're gone? So are your leads.

Now, here's what *not* to do:

- Don't start with your bio.

I love you, and I'm sure you're very accomplished. But no one came to hear a dramatic reading of your résumé. They came because they have a problem, and hope you can help solve it. So before you rattle off your credentials, start by proving you understand them. Make it clear: "I see you. I get what you're struggling with. And I've got something you need."

Next up: structure.

Back in that Zumba class, I didn't need an interpretive dance showcase. I needed one simple move I could repeat without causing a scene.

Same goes for your talk.

- Do organize your message around one to three key takeaways.

People don't remember fifteen points. Heck, they barely remember their passwords.

Clarity wins. If your audience can leave with just one powerful idea that makes them think, "I can do this," you've done your job.

- Don't info-dump.

This isn't a TED Talk, a masterclass, and a group therapy session. Trying to cram everything in doesn't make you helpful; it makes you forgettable.

Now let's talk about who your message is for.

- Do speak to their pain points.

If you're not tapping into what keeps your audience up at night, you're just giving a nice little speech, and nice doesn't sell. People are walking around with real problems. They're overwhelmed. Frustrated. Stuck. And they're dying for someone to finally say the thing they've been thinking, but haven't had the words for.

Be that person.

Speak straight to the ache.
Say what no one else is saying.
Show them you get it deeply.

- Don't make it about you.

You're not the star. They are. You're the guide. The person with the flashlight showing them the way out of the tunnel.

What happens when you stop trying to impress and start trying to serve? That's when the magic happens. That's when the room leans in. That's when people say, "She's talking to me." And that's when your message becomes more than words. It becomes the solution they've been waiting for.

Building a business shouldn't feel like surviving a Zumba class.

But for most entrepreneurs, it does.

You're sweating, spinning in circles, flailing your way through every new strategy the internet throws at you. "Post more!" "Rebrand!" "Try this funnel!" And while you're trying to salsa left, the rest of the world feels like it's cha-cha-cha-ing right past you with clients, cash, and clarity.

You're not lazy. You're not broken. You're just exhausted from trying to do everything, except the one thing that actually moves the needle.

Speaking.

Not the kind where you ramble and hope someone's listening. I'm talking about speaking that connects, converts, and puts you in a category of one.

The moment I stopped cold-calling campuses and started stepping on stages, my business shifted fast. And not because I had better branding or a bigger following. But because I had something to say, and I finally found the right room to say it in.

That's what I want for you.

Because here's the thing: Your business doesn't need another trend. It needs traction.

You've got expertise. You've got solutions. You just need more people to know it and trust it fast.

Speaking does that.

It's the move that turns chaos into clarity. The move that takes you from overlooked to unforgettable. The move that, once you nail it, lets you finally add that "flavor" everyone keeps talking about, without knocking out a row of innocent bystanders along the way.

You don't have to keep dancing in circles, hoping something sticks.

You just need to step up, speak out, and show your audience what you're really made of.

You've already got the rhythm. Now let's turn it into results.

Be the dynamic, problem-solving speaker. And let them see you.

ALISSA CRABTREE

Alissa Crabtree is a speaker coach and former educator who helps business owners turn their expertise into lead-generating presentations. With nearly 20 years of experience in teaching and adult coaching, she combines proven frameworks with personalized strategy to help her clients speak with confidence, clarity, and purpose. Through her coaching, entrepreneurs stop winging it on stage and start converting audiences into clients.

www.instagram.com/crabtree_coaching_collab/

THE SWIFT EFFECT: WHY SPEAKING UP BUILDS INFLUENCE, LOYALTY, AND LEGACY

Melissa Creede, Celebrity & Executive Coach

I'm just going to come out and say it.

I love Taylor Swift.

I admit it, without qualifiers and without apology, and not because of her music. Not because of the glitter, the stadium tours, or the sold-out vinyl pressings, although all of that is amazing.

I love Taylor Swift because she uses her platform not just to entertain, but to lead.

Taylor Swift is a masterclass in *values-based influence*. She has built an empire, yes, but she has also built something more important. She has shown us that leadership does not require a title, that being a changemaker does not require permission, that using your voice can be a strategy, not just for impact, but for growth.

When Taylor began speaking out about misogyny, about sexism, about the things she once stayed quiet about, she didn't lose everything.

In fact, her fame and impact skyrocketed.

New fans, deeper trust, greater relevance. She gained people who didn't even know her music, but knew her values, and chose her because of them.

They became her army, because she became their voice.

And if you are a celebrity, executive, entrepreneur, or artist, *you can do the same.*

This is not a call to become a Swiftie. She doesn't need my help with that, anyway. It is a call to recognize that *influence aligned with purpose becomes power.* It is the kind of power that shapes culture, builds loyalty, drives movements, and yes, grows brands and businesses.

Let's talk about why.

First: Alignment is magnetic.

When you stand for something, your people will find you. That is true whether you are on stage, in a boardroom, on a set, or in a C-suite. People want to buy from, work for, follow, and champion those who reflect their values.

In fact, 94 percent of millennial and Gen Z consumers prefer to buy from organizations and brands that demonstrate strong social responsibility[**], and as the younger generations gain buying power and expect more from the people they support, the stakes are only rising.

The world is noisy, the world is burning, the world is scrolling, and in that chaos, *authenticity cuts through.*

It is not just good ethics. It is good business.

[**] CSR Window. *Demand for CSR Among Gen Z and Millennials 2023.* CSR Window Impact Lab, March 2023. https://csrwindow.com

Let's look at some proof.

When Taylor Swift encouraged her fans to register to vote in 2019, voter registration spiked by more than 1,200 percent in a single hour.

When Rihanna launched Fenty Beauty with a then-radical commitment to inclusive shades and representation, she did not just make headlines. *She changed the beauty industry*. And it made her a billionaire.

When Elizabeth Taylor stepped into the void during the AIDS crisis, long before it was seen as safe or popular, she became more than a celebrity. *She became a legacy*.

When Costco chose to double down on its commitments to diversity in a moment when competitors were walking theirs back, it gained almost eight million new customer visits in a single month.

This is what I want you to understand: *Values are not just something nice to have. They are strategic assets*.

They create market share. They generate relevance. They future-proof your platform.

Still, I get it.

Maybe you are thinking, "I'm really busy; now isn't the right time." Or, "I'll speak up once I hit a million followers." Or, "What if I say the wrong thing?" Or, "What if I lose fans, clients, or career opportunities?"

Those fears are real. They are human, and they are familiar to everyone I work with, from founders to executives to entertainers.

But here is what I tell them: Speaking up isn't what you do after you succeed.

It's not the reward for arriving. It's the reason you get there.

Because when your platform reflects your purpose, your audience grows. Not randomly, but intentionally. You attract people who believe in you. Who stay with you. Who don't just click or consume; they commit.

And this kind of loyalty cannot be bought. It is earned.

So how do you start?

Start by asking yourself:

What matters to me?
What is the issue I can't unsee anymore?
What injustice makes me pause mid-scroll?
What topic makes me want to slam the table and say, "Why isn't someone doing something about this?"

That is your spark. That is your direction.

So what now? Here are a few things to keep in mind:

1. *Your purpose, or the causes you align with, must be authentic, or it simply won't resonate.* This isn't something your public relations (PR) team, your marketing department, or your internal communications staff can script. You need someone trained to help you uncover what truly matters to *you*, even if it's not what people expect or what your brand has done before. And you should explore this in a confidential, sometimes messy way *before* you're ready to go public with it.

2. *You need a strategy.* This isn't about reacting to headlines, waiting for the perfect moment to post, or trying to fire up your team with a motivational burst. It's about aligning your message, your platform, and your goals with clarity and intention. Strategy doesn't just

protect your voice, it sharpens it. It amplifies your reach and anchors your integrity.

3. *You need a personal champion*. You need someone who can support you through the self-doubt, the second-guessing, the imposter syndrome, the external noise and the critics, especially when fear takes over. There is a reason why the most successful and impactful leaders and public figures have personal coaches. You need someone who wants everything *for* you and nothing *from* you. That's the role I play.

This is what I help my clients do: quiet the noise, name their purpose, clarify their causes, connect with their people and community, and lead with power and confidence.

And here's what most people miss:

We overthink this. We imagine we need a personal origin story or expert credentials to care deeply about something. But you don't need to be the face of a community to support it. You don't need to have all the answers. *You don't need permission to care*.

You need a heart and a voice.

Once you have that purpose, that heart, that voice, it infuses everything you do: what you talk about, content you share, speeches you give, vision you lead, decisions you make. It becomes part of who you are, and that is what makes you compelling. *That* is what draws others to you.

Because leadership, *real leadership*, isn't about perfection. It is about courage.

You will get it wrong sometimes. You will stumble.

You might be criticized. But none of that is failure. It is part of the work.

You cannot make meaningful change without making someone uncomfortable. Sometimes the discomfort will be theirs. Sometimes it will be yours. But that is what disruption looks like.

When you speak up, you will not be for everyone. But you will be unmistakably clear for the people who matter most.

And that is how *movements begin*.

Think about the people you admire most. The ones whose careers transcend roles or trends. The ones who mean something to their fans, their followers, their employees, their colleagues, their audiences.

It is not just what they do. It is what they stand for.

They are known. They are trusted. They are chosen.

You do not need to be famous to do this well. But if you are, you have even more responsibility and opportunity.

This is where I come in.

I help people, people like you, clarify their values, choose causes that are authentic and heartfelt, and navigate this work with care, credibility, and strategy. I help you align your internal compass with your public voice.

Because these issues are nuanced and the stakes are high. You do not want performative activism or shallow statements.

You want *impact. Integrity. Intentionality.*

And sometimes, you just need a *champion*, someone who believes in what you are doing and helps you say it well.

I believe in you. I believe you are here for a reason. And I believe your voice can change the world, starting with the corner of it you already influence.

But I also know this: The hardest part is often the first step.

You do not need to map the entire journey right now. You just need to take that first action. Make that first call. Say that first truth.

Think of it like a hike. It is not just about reaching the top of the mountain or getting a great post for your socials. It is about feeling *awestruck. Alive. Part of something bigger than yourself.*

That is what this is, a hike toward purpose.

Listen to that voice inside you. The one that has been trying to get your attention. The one that says, *"This matters to me."*

That voice is not noise. It is a signal.

And it is time to follow it.

Because *a legacy is not something you leave behind.*

It is something you *live out loud, on purpose, every day.*

And *every movement begins with someone who dared to care and said so out loud.*

Let that someone be you.

Just start.

MELISSA CREEDE

Melissa Creede helps executives, celebrities, and entrepreneurs use their voice for meaningful change. Formerly an executive working on complex global issues, she now coaches influential leaders, including those from Fortune 50 companies, to align their values with their visibility, make an impact, and lead with purpose.

She is the international bestselling author of Beyond Your Inbox: Intentional Leadership in a Distracted World.

Melissa has worked and played in 60 countries: installing solar panels in Argentina, hiking in Nepal, Kenya, and Pakistan, and backpacking across Asia, Europe, and Eastern Africa.

She brings bold vision, practical strategy, deep heart, and a global lens to every leader she serves.

www.LeadWithMelissa.ca/fame-is-fleeting

LEADING THROUGH THE MESS: HOW TO SHIFT STRESS, ALIGN ENERGY, AND UNLOCK TEAM PERFORMANCE

Alycia Diggs-Chavis

You walk into a meeting and think, *Did I just land on the set of Survivor?*

Your team looks shell-shocked. One person's panicking, like you asked them to eat a live bug. Someone else is fighting back tears. And you? You're smack in the middle of the chaos, wondering how you went from leading a team to trying not to extinguish your own torch.

It's a mess. But here's the twist: If your team feels like a reality show gone sideways, your leadership energy may be part of the reason.

I say that without judgment. Leadership can be exhausting. You've tried everything—books, podcasts, strategies. You push harder, hoping something sticks. But despite your effort, nothing's really changing. Your results are flat. Your team's disconnected. And you're stuck asking, *What's wrong with them?*

But what if that's the wrong question?

What if the problem isn't your team?

What if it's *you*?

Before you throw this book across the room—hear me out. This isn't about blame. It's about awareness. Because leadership isn't just about what you *say*—it's about what you *bring*.

There's a concept I call **The Leadership Energy Connection.** It's the recognition that **your energy doesn't stay contained—it echoes through your entire team.**

It's less like a solo performance and more like dropping a stone in water—**every thought, mood, and mindset create ripples.**

When you're centered and aligned, your team syncs up.

But when your inner world is in chaos?

That ripple turns into a ripple—and **your team feels it, whether they realize it or not.**

You've seen it happen. **Miscommunication** creeps in. A simple email turns into a tangled mess of replies, confusion, and office drama. Then comes the **mayhem**—shifting priorities, chaotic rollouts, mixed messages. And before long? Everyone's just trying to make it to Friday without imploding.

That's when the deeper kind of **exhaustion** sets in. Not "I need a nap" tired. I'm talking soul-level burnout. And when people are burned out, everything **stagnates**—innovation, creativity, even basic communication. They're no longer working toward anything— they're just surviving. And finally, the real killer—**skepticism.** When a leader is frazzled, reactive, and constantly shifting gears, people stop trusting the direction. They start questioning you. And once that happens, motivation and commitment go out the window.

When leaders are reactive and unclear, trust starts to erode. And when trust breaks down, motivation goes with it.

Miscommunication. Mayhem. Exhaustion. Stagnation. Skepticism.

That's the **MESS**. But here's the good news: The **MESS** is fixable.

Not with another meeting. Not with a better calendar app. But by starting with you. Because when you clean up your own energy, everything around you starts to shift. You communicate more clearly. You make decisions with confidence. You stop leading from panic and start leading with presence.

Your team feels that shift—and they rise with you.

This is where I come in.

I help leaders reset their energy, reclaim their clarity, and realign their leadership. I blend strategy with energy work—because let's be honest, you can't separate the two. You can't lead powerfully if you're dragging around stress and self-doubt like an extra carry-on.

What I do is part ancient wisdom, part real-world leadership coaching. I help people get unstuck—from relationships, careers, finances, and leadership blocks. Because if something feels off in your life or your work, chances are your energy has something to do with it.

It's not about being perfect. It's about finding your flow.

And suddenly? Everything starts working again.

I want to touch on something we don't talk about enough: **energy and balance.**

We all know that person who brags, *"I was up at 4 a.m., already answering emails, hit the gym, ran a meeting, solved a crisis, and I haven't eaten since Tuesday!"*—and somehow, we're supposed to be impressed.

But let me ask you this: When was the last time running on fumes led to great leadership? Because what's really happening isn't high performance—it's burnout.

That's why creating *sustainable* success matters. When leaders push past their limits without refueling and resetting their energy, it sets a silent standard. Before long, you've got an entire workplace of people pretending to be productive while secretly fantasizing about quitting during the Monday meeting. And then what? Absenteeism rises. Turnover spikes. Productivity tanks.

But I've seen what happens when leaders start taking balance seriously—when they rest, reset, and model that behavior for others. If you want success that lasts—for you and your people—you've got to stop glorifying grind culture. Start modeling what real balance looks like.

And yes …maybe even get a full night's sleep.

Now I've had the privilege of working with leaders across industries— from government to education to healthcare to corporate—and one thing is always true: The energy you carry sets the emotional tone of your organization. Period.

I often lead exercises where leaders physically feel their own energy for the first time. Some of them are skeptical at first, but once they sense the shift, once they *experience* the difference between stressed energy and grounded energy—it changes everything. It's like someone handed them the missing piece of the leadership puzzle.

And it doesn't stop there. Once you understand that energy is a leadership tool—not just a wellness practice—you realize how powerful you really are. Because when you manage your energy, you're not just helping yourself. You're creating the conditions for your team to thrive.

That's why I created one particular stress release blueprint called **Energetic Edge**. Stress isn't just a nuisance; it's a leadership liability. We wear stress like a badge of honor. But burnout doesn't make you a better leader. It just makes you a ticking time bomb.

So managing your energy actually gives you a strategic edge.

The blueprint I teach is as simple as breathing, and anything but ordinary. It is a precision technique that dissolves stress on the spot. No waiting, no guesswork. It is a survival tool for modern leaders. And the best part? It takes less than three minutes. I've had CEOs tell me that those three minutes changed the course of their day—and sometimes their entire approach to leadership.

Because when your body feels safe, your brain works better. You communicate more clearly. You listen more deeply. You make decisions from your *higher self*, not your fight-or-flight response.

And that brings us to one of the most powerful tools in your leadership arsenal—your **intuition**.

How often have you *known* something deep down ...only to overthink it into oblivion? You had a gut feeling, but your brain barged in and demanded data, spreadsheets, a committee vote, and a pros-and-cons list before you could take action.

We've been taught to treat intuition like it's some flaky, unreliable thing. But in reality, it's one of the most efficient, effective guidance systems you have.

I once stood at a major life crossroads: go to grad school and follow the "smart" path or join the Peace Corps and follow the pull. Every logical voice around me said, "grad school." But my inner knowing said otherwise.

I chose the Peace Corps. And it changed the trajectory of my life in all the best ways.

Leadership is full of those moments. When the data says one thing, but your gut says another. When the team wants to move in one direction, but you don't agree with them. Those are the moments that separate reactive leaders from transformative ones.

So the question becomes: Are you willing to get quiet enough to listen?

When you lead from your higher self—the part of you that already *knows*—decision-making gets faster, easier, and more aligned. And your team? They trust you more. Because they can feel the difference between confidence and guesswork.

Now, none of this works unless you build it into something sustainable.

That's why I help leaders create rhythms that support *sustainable success*. Not success that requires constant sacrifice, but success that feels grounded, regenerative, and *repeatable*.

You know that person who brags about doing emails at 4 a.m., hasn't taken a vacation in two years, and thinks burnout is a personality trait? Yeah—don't be that leader.

True success doesn't come from overextension. It comes from *alignment*. From knowing when to push and when to pause. From setting the tone for your team, not with frantic urgency but with calm, steady clarity.

I worked with a principal who came into a session completely fried. He had just been punched by a student. He was out of options. Paralyzed. I didn't give him a checklist or a pep talk. I asked if we could go off-script. I did a remote energy clearing. Two days later, he was back—centered, clear, ready to lead again.

If you had told me years ago that I'd be standing in front of rooms full of high-powered leaders, talking about energy work, singing bowls, and sacred geometry—I would've laughed you out of the building. That kind of thing belonged at yoga retreats, not leadership conferences.

And yet ... here we are.

Because what I've learned—what I've *lived*—is that no amount of strategy can compensate for misaligned energy. You can have the sharpest mind, the best team, the most well-oiled systems—but if the leader is burned out, disconnected, or spiraling internally, none of it sticks. It all starts to wobble.

I've seen it in companies. I've seen it in families.

I didn't set out to "convince" anyone. I just did the work. I focused on myself—my healing, my alignment, my energy. And without ever preaching or pushing, the people closest to me began to shift. That's when I realized: If this is what happens in a home, imagine what happens in a *team*.

Because energy isn't just personal—it's contagious. It's the silent language that speaks louder than any team meeting or leadership memo. When you shift your frequency, the people around you begin to rise to meet it. And that's exactly what this journey is. It's not about finding the perfect solution out there. It's about awakening the clarity already within you.

So what if you stopped running and started aligning? What if your most powerful leadership tool wasn't your hustle—but your presence?

The truth is, when you do this work—when you shift internally—your leadership becomes magnetic. Your team starts responding differently. Challenges feel less overwhelming. Decisions come more easily. And you stop surviving the chaos and start shaping the culture.

That's not just good leadership. That's *transformational* leadership.

So if you're feeling stuck, stretched, scattered—or just know deep down that there's a better way—this is your invitation.

Not to fix everything overnight. Not to become someone else.

But to *return* to the most powerful version of yourself. The one who leads not from pressure, but from power. Not from survival, but from clarity.

Your team doesn't need you to be perfect.

They need you to be present. To be real. To be *aligned*.

Because when you shift—when you truly step into that energy—everything changes.

Your meetings aren't war zones. Your strategies actually work. Your culture comes alive. And your people? They thrive.

Why? Because they felt the shift in *you*.

So let's stop chasing fixes and start embodying solutions.

Let's lead differently.

Let's lead *brilliantly*.

And it all starts right here—with you.

ALYCIA DIGGS-CHAVIS

As founder of BlueViolet Energy, Alycia Diggs-Chavis is a trusted advisor to leaders who no longer settle for surface-level solutions. A Harvard graduate, Executive Advisor, Certified Master Energy Healer, Emotion-Mind-Energy™ Practitioner, and former corporate leader who managed multimillion-dollar operations, she now partners with high-performing entrepreneurs and C-suite executives to sharpen their edge and access their untapped genius. Her work blends intuitive precision and targeted energetic recalibration to elevate decision-making and bottom-line results. For leaders who've outgrown traditional coaching and want outcomes that finally match their potential, Alycia delivers transformation at the highest level.

www.linkedin.com/in/AlyciaDiggsChavis

THE OXYGEN ADVANTAGE (YOU NEVER LEARNED IN MED SCHOOL): THE UNTAUGHT THERAPY THAT HEALS FASTER, GROWS REVENUE, AND SETS YOU APART

Nicole Garrett

Apparently, I'm just like the lead character from that old TV show *Bones*. That's what my team tells me.

"Totally you," they said. "You're Dr. Temperance Brennan."

If you've never seen it, Dr. Brennan is a forensic anthropologist who solves FBI cases by analyzing human remains. She's brilliant, blunt, hyper-rational—and maybe a little emotionally unavailable. Everything is evidence. Logic. Data.

Naturally, I took it as a compliment. But then I had to ask: "Wait, are you saying I'm … difficult?"

They laughed harder than I'd like to admit. "No, no—it's a compliment. Mostly."

That comparison stuck. Because what they were really saying is: I might be a little too clinical. A little too textbook. Sometimes my words feel more like a journal abstract than a human conversation.

So today, I'm trying something different. A little less Temperance Brennan. A little more … human.

Let's see how this goes.

Knock, knock.
Who's there?
O2.
O2 who?
O2 bad if you don't open a chamber—you're gonna need it!

Did someone groan? Yeah, I heard that. But here's what's not a joke: Hyperbaric oxygen therapy isn't just powerful—it's profitable.

If you're a health practitioner and you add it to your practice, two things happen: Your patients heal faster and your bottom line gets stronger.

I know what you're thinking. You've already got a practice. You're busy. You're seeing patients. And sure, the revenue looks solid—on paper.

But between staff, equipment, overhead, and insurance, your take-home isn't exactly what people imagine. You're working hard … but where's the payoff?

Now imagine adding something that helps patients recover faster, reduces complications, and doesn't require more hours from you. Imagine getting better outcomes *and* better margins.

That's what hyperbaric oxygen therapy does.

And if you're wondering why you didn't learn this in med school, you're not alone. Most physicians get exactly one hour—one—on hyperbarics during all four years of training. If you rotated through a hospital with it, maybe you saw it during residency.

But for the most part? It's off the radar.

That doesn't mean it's fringe. Hyperbaric oxygen therapy is FDA-approved, backed by research, and used in hospitals around the world. It reduces inflammation, accelerates healing, and improves surgical outcomes. It's not experimental. It's just underutilized.

And it's not just about the patients—it's about you. Your reputation. Your results. Your revenue.

When your patients heal faster, scar less, and avoid complications—you look like the doctor who makes the impossible happen.

And that changes everything.

Because when other doctors refer to you, they don't send easy cases. They send disasters. The patients no one else can help.

But when *those* patients improve? When they bounce back faster, with fewer side effects, and better outcomes?

You become the go-to.

Financially, the upside is real.

And here's the best part: you: You don't do the work. I do.

I handle the OSHA regulations. The Medicare certifications. The NFPA compliance. I bring the equipment, the build-out, the protocols, even the staff. You don't need to hire a technician—I employ them.

You just provide the space and approve the plan.

And no, I don't disappear after installation. I stay in it with you. I manage it. I keep it running. Because I've seen what this therapy can do, and I believe in it.

This is a partnership. One where you do what you do best—care for your patients—and I handle everything behind the scenes.

Why wouldn't you want that?

If you're still unsure, think of it like this: Adding hyperbarics is like upgrading from a flip phone to a smartphone. The old way still works. But why settle for less when you could have better outcomes, happier patients, and more money?

Knock, knock.
Who's there?
O2.
O2 who?
O2 bad you haven't added hyperbarics yet—you're leaving healing and revenue on the table.

Okay, okay—I couldn't resist.

But now that I've got your attention, let's go deeper into what makes this therapy work—and why it could be the smartest decision you make for your practice.

Let's start with a little truth bomb: Not all hyperbaric oxygen therapy is created equal.

There's the real thing—100 percent oxygen at 2.0 ATA or higher—and then there's what I like to call the "mall massage" version. You know the one. Looks relaxing, sounds legit, but doesn't actually deliver what people need.

That's what's happening with a lot of those soft- and low-pressure chambers. They might look the part, but they aren't equipped to create real physiological change. People go in, expect results, and walk away disappointed.

And when patients don't get results, they don't just blame the provider—they blame the therapy itself.

But when people get the right protocol, in the right setting, with the right equipment? The results are undeniable.

That's why I'm obsessive about doing this the right way. Because the right way works.

And when it comes to safety? Let's not mess around.

Hyperbarics is powerful. That means it also has to be precise. This isn't something you DIY. It requires medical-grade equipment, trained technicians, and strict safety protocols. You can't fake it.

I've seen clinics try to cut corners. They think a basic chamber and a few laminated instructions are enough. They're not. Not even close.

When people cut corners, things go wrong—and the entire field takes the hit.

But when it's done correctly? Safely? Consistently? That's when the magic happens. That's when you see healing that defies expectations.

Like new blood vessels.

Yes—actual new blood vessels.

Hyperbaric oxygen therapy is the only treatment we know of that *grows* new ones. It stimulates angiogenesis—regenerating pathways in tissues that have been damaged, blocked, or deprived of oxygen.

That's not symptom management. That's repair.

Think about how many treatments just mask pain or slow progression. This one builds something new. Something permanent.

And the process behind it? Surprisingly simple.

Imagine a can of soda. When sealed, carbon dioxide is dissolved in the liquid. Open it—and the pressure drops, releasing the gas.

In the chamber, we do the reverse. We increase atmospheric pressure so oxygen dissolves directly into the blood plasma—not just the red blood cells. That means oxygen can reach places red blood cells can't get to. Crushed arteries. Damaged veins. Blocked vessels.

That's why I've seen dusky, purple limbs turn pink again inside the chamber. Why I've seen amputation cases reversed. Why I've watched recovery times shrink.

Because oxygen is finally getting where it needs to go.

And while we're at it, let's talk about inflammation.

Inflammation is the medical equivalent of stepping on a Lego. Small. Sneaky. Capable of ruining everything.

It starts off minor—maybe a little joint stiffness, some digestive issues, a bit of fatigue. But ignore it, and it spreads.

Inflammation is behind most chronic illnesses. And until you deal with it, you're just treating symptoms.

Hyperbarics doesn't just reduce inflammation—it pulls it back enough to expose the real root. That's when you can figure out what's actually going on.

I've had patients with Crohn's disease who were constantly flaring. Once we calmed the inflammation with hyperbarics, we could finally identify the trigger—gluten, dairy, stress—and get them into remission.

That's game-changing. Because when your patients get real relief, they don't just come back. They send everyone they know.

Which brings us to your business.

Because it's one thing to make money. It's another to keep it.

We all know someone who makes a lot, but somehow always feels broke. That's the difference between gross revenue and net revenue.

Hyperbarics doesn't just boost your top line—it protects your bottom line. It's high-value care with low operational cost. Once it's running, it runs efficiently. Patients see the results. They feel better. They return.

And when you're known as the doctor who gets results no one else can? You build trust. And trust builds practices.

I've had doctors send me patients they thought were lost causes—brain injuries, non-healing wounds, severe trauma. One of them called me and said, "We sent you a vegetable. Now they're living independently again. How?!"

Simple. Oxygen.

We just change how we deliver it.

That's why I'm here. Because this isn't just about creating another revenue stream—it's about delivering a level of care most people never even imagined was possible.

But here's the frustrating part: Insurance usually won't cover it unless the patient falls into one of fourteen very specific categories. Most don't.

That means thousands of dollars out of pocket, and most people can't swing it. Which is exactly why I built my own center—to make it accessible.

Now, I'm helping other doctors do the same. And not just to run a business—but to actually change lives.

I started by saying I wanted to sound a little less like a medical encyclopedia and a little more ... human.

And sure, I threw in a few jokes, tried to keep things light. But here's what really matters:

Hyperbaric oxygen therapy changes lives. It accelerates healing. It reduces complications. It helps people recover when no one else could help them. And yes—it generates real revenue.

So even if you're still deciding whether I sound more like a genius, a mad scientist, or just that woman who really, really loves oxygen—it's beside the point.

The point is this is real. It's ready. And it can help your patients—and your practice—in ways you've probably never seen before.

And if you're hesitating—if you're wondering, "Is this too complicated?" or "What if I don't fully get it yet?"—I'll say this:

You don't have to understand every technical detail. That's my job.

You just have to be willing to explore the possibility that there's something out there that could make your work easier, your outcomes better, and your business stronger.

The worst thing that happens? We talk, and you decide it's not the right fit right now.

The best thing?

You change lives. Yours included.

Because when you add hyperbarics, you don't just add another service. You add a superpower.

You become the doctor patients rave about. The one who healed what no one else could. The one whose results speak for themselves.

All without adding hours to your schedule or chaos to your clinic.

So take a breath. Literally.

Then let's talk about how to make that breath work for you.

Okay—one last time, and then I promise I'll stop.

Knock, knock.
Who's there?
O_2.
O_2 who?
O_2 be the doctor known for healing the impossible *and* making more money?

Couldn't help myself.

But if you're still reading? Maybe you're ready to answer that knock.

NICOLE GARRETT

Nicole Garrett, CHT, founder of Under Pressure, brings a wealth of experience in hyperbaric medicine, having nearly two decades in the field. With a background in commercial diving and dive medicine, Nicole's career began at UC San Diego's hyperbaric chamber, where she treated complex cases such as crush injuries, air gas embolisms, decompression illness, diabetic wounds, and the effects of radiation for cancer treatment. She played a pivotal role in a Department of Defense study on traumatic brain injuries and went on to establish UCSD's second multiplace hyperbaric facility in Encinitas, CA. Her expertise extends to designing and launching hyperbaric facilities nationwide, training physicians and staff, and consulting globally on hyperbaric safety and operations. Nicole's leadership at Under Pressure reflects her commitment to using advanced hyperbaric therapies to optimize patient outcomes.

www.UnderPressure.com

INVISIBLE LUGGAGE: UNPACKING THE BIAS YOU DON'T KNOW YOU'RE CARRYING

Teresa Gregory

Ten seconds.

That's all it takes for someone to make a snap judgment. Before you speak, before you introduce yourself, someone's brain has already decided something about you. Maybe it's your height, your hair, the way you walk, or some half-memory you trigger. Doesn't matter what it is; the brain pulls from its files and fills in the blanks.

We all do it. It's instinct. It's bias.

Unconscious bias, to be exact.

And while it's often automatic and unintentional, it still affects how we treat others—and how we see ourselves. Good news: once you're aware of it, you can interrupt it. You can shift it. You can go from passive habit to conscious choice. That's where real leadership begins.

Because if we're honest, most of us aren't walking into work saying, "I want to be a leader today." We're thinking things like, "Why didn't I get the promotion?" or "Why don't they see what I bring to the table?" The frustration underneath all of that? It's about control. Or rather, the feeling that we don't have it.

And if you're in management, it's not like you're fantasizing about building a dream team. You're thinking, "If these people could just get along, we might actually hit our numbers, and I might finally get that raise." I hear it all the time: "We need team building." But what they really mean is, "We need to hit our targets without the drama."

So we try trust falls. Icebreakers. Personality quizzes. But here's the truth: none of that works if you don't understand what's really driving disconnection. And often, it's bias.

Not always the big, obvious kind. I'm talking about the everyday kind. The kind that shows up when you assume someone's lazy because they're late or disengaged because they're quiet. The kind that makes you misread silence as attitude. Or earbuds as disrespect. That's bias, too. And it's quietly shaping how we lead—or don't.

I've worked with plenty of managers who say, "My team's great individually, but they're not working together." That's usually the moment I tell them, "You don't have a team problem. You have a bias problem."

When you start to understand how people operate, not just what they do, but how they do it, you begin to lead. And once you can see the blind spots, once you can name the assumptions, everything changes.

That's what I help people do.

I didn't start out coaching executives or running corporate training. My first job was collecting carts in the Target parking lot. And yes, dodging runaway carts in a red vest teaches you more about human nature than most management books.

But I wasn't content just doing the job. I noticed a gap: there was no front-end training. So, I created it. Sent it to corporate. That program became the model for cashier training nationwide. That's when I learned something crucial: leadership starts when you act, not when someone gives you permission.

Later, I pivoted out of accounting school, yes, I love calculus, no shame, and into human resources and organizational behavior. That led me to a sales and marketing job, then into recruiting, and eventually to Microsoft.

At Microsoft, I onboarded CFOs. Not just one—thirteen of them. I helped restructure teams, rebuild departments, and coach leaders at the highest level. I was instrumental in creating the Finance Academy to help professionals build not just their technical skills, but the soft ones too—the ones that move teams forward.

That's where I saw it: the difference between managing and leading. A manager checks boxes. A leader sees people.

And what kept showing up, every time, was bias.

Bias kept teams from trusting. From collaborating. From promoting the right people. From making smart decisions. So, I got to work building programs that helped people see the bias, unpack it, and lead beyond it.

I'm a certified Myers-Briggs practitioner, a developer of over 400 trainings, and a consultant to companies like Microsoft, Boeing, and Kaiser Permanente. But more than anything, I'm someone who helps teams connect and helps individuals finally step into leadership.

Because the shift from team member to team leader? It doesn't start with a title.

It starts with seeing what's in your way.

Ready to look?

Let's start with the simplest truth: we all have bias.

Even if you don't think you do. Even if you pride yourself on being fair. That voice in your head that tells you who to trust, who to avoid, who's doing great and who's slacking? That's bias. And most of the time, you don't even know it's happening.

Take something as basic as your morning coffee. You probably reach for the same brand every day. That's not just habit, that's familiarity. That's bias formed by exposure. Your brain has experienced something multiple times, and now it says, "This is good. This is safe. This is mine."

That's how bias works. The more you're exposed to something: an idea, a person, a product, the more your brain favors it. Not because it's better, but because it's known. Our brains love shortcuts. Familiar equals safe. Unfamiliar equals risky. And just like that, we're making decisions based on what's comfortable, not what's accurate or right or best.

It happens at the office, too. You've worked with someone like Sarah before, so you assume this new Sarah will be just like her. Or someone doesn't greet you in the hallway, and your brain decides, "They're rude." But maybe they were just focused. Maybe they didn't see you. Bias steps in and tells a story before you even ask the question.

And here's the kicker: bias doesn't just come from repetition. It also comes from deeper places like faith, education, beliefs, and past experiences. These are the lenses you look through every day without even knowing it.

If you grew up with certain values, you see the world through that lens. If your education emphasized certain ideas, those ideas shape how you evaluate new information. If you had a bad experience with a boss who micromanaged, you might bristle at every manager after that, whether they deserve it or not.

Even things like beliefs about introverts, fashion choices, or someone's tone of voice—these tiny inputs form and trigger mental shortcuts. And the more you let those shortcuts run the show, the harder it becomes to see what's really in front of you.

It's like walking around with sunglasses on and forgetting you're wearing them.

And then there's the big trap: mistaking intention for impact.

You meant it as a joke. They didn't laugh. You were trying to help. They got defensive. You thought it was harmless. They found it hurtful. We've all been there.

The problem isn't just that you got it wrong; it's that we're conditioned to defend our intention instead of acknowledging the impact. "I didn't mean it that way" becomes a shield. But leadership isn't about being right. It's about being responsible. When you're willing to own the impact, even when it didn't match your intent, you build trust.

That leads us to the hardest truth of all: removing bias takes work.

You can't just flip a switch and decide to see clearly. You must retrain your brain. And that starts with identifying your triggers.

A trigger is any moment that sends you into autopilot thinking. Maybe someone shows up late, and your brain immediately labels them unreliable. Or someone speaks with hesitation, and you assume they lack confidence. Those are triggers. And if you don't catch them, they steer your judgment.

The work is in noticing. Interrupting. Reframing.

You say to yourself, "Wait—am I reacting to this person, or to something they remind me of?" You pause and ask, "Is there another possible story here?" That moment of questioning is powerful. Because the second you disrupt the automatic judgment, you give yourself space to choose differently.

And yes, it's hard. It takes repetition. You'll get it wrong sometimes. But that's not failure. That's growth. You're not trying to erase your bias. You're learning to manage it.

Think of it like carrying a backpack. You've had it since you were born. It's full of stories, assumptions, and experiences. Some are helpful, some are not. You can't throw it away. But you *can* stop letting it run your life. That's the difference between reacting and leading.

When you understand what's in your backpack—when you see your bias and make a different choice—you lead with clarity. With empathy. With intention.

And that's the kind of leadership that changes everything.

So let's circle back to where we began: those first ten seconds.

You saw me. Your brain reacted. Maybe it was my hair. My posture. A memory I triggered that had nothing to do with me. And your mind filled in the blanks. That's not judgment. That's just being human.

But now? You're aware of it. And that awareness is where real power lives.

Because the goal isn't to never have a bias. That's impossible. The goal is to recognize it when it shows up, and then choose differently. That choice, made repeatedly, is what turns you into a leader people trust.

Leadership isn't about your title. It's about how you make others feel. It's about creating a space where people feel seen, respected, and valued for who they are, not just for what they produce.

And when you start leading from that place?

Your team changes. Your culture changes. You change.

People stop walking on eggshells. They start speaking up. They trust you. They perform at their best because they know you see them clearly; they will sense that you are not looking at them through a lens of assumptions, but with genuine curiosity and care.

Maya Angelou said, *"People will forget what you said, people will forget what you did, but people will never forget how you made them feel."* That's what this work is about. How you make people feel when they're around you.

So here's your challenge.

Look in your backpack. What stories are still influencing how you show up? What snap judgments are running in the background? What's getting in your way?

You don't need to fix everything overnight. You just need to start noticing. Catch a trigger. Question a thought. Be open to seeing someone—or yourself—differently.

That's the shift.

That's the start of the leader you're becoming.

And if you're ready to do this work, if you're done waiting for someone else to hand you a promotion, a raise, or recognition, then know this:

You don't need permission.

You're already capable. You just need to clear the path.

Let's unpack that backpack. Let's shift the stories. Let's lead like it matters—because it does.

Your future team is counting on you.

And frankly?

So are you.

TERESA GREGORY

Teresa Gregory is a leadership strategist, speaker, and mentor who empowers professionals to grow into high-impact leaders. Grounded in real-world experience, she champions transformational leadership built on trust, respect, and self-awareness. She offers practical, research-based strategies to help leaders at every level elevate their influence, inspire teams, and achieve lasting success.

www.SquaredSuccess.com

BOSSY WOO® RISING: THE FIERCE NEW WAY TO ALIGN, ACT, AND OWN YOUR INTUITION

Valerie Holden

Ever feel like the universe is trying to get your attention?

Like one day you look in the mirror and think, *Is this really my life?* You've followed the rules, checked the boxes, done the things—and yet, something still feels off. Like you're living a version of life that looks good on paper but doesn't feel like you.

Now imagine someone flashes a badge and says, "You're under arrest for abandoning your soul's purpose."

That someone would be me.

I spent years as a police officer. So yes, I know how to arrest someone. But now? Now I'm more interested in setting people free—from burnout, from self-doubt, from the invisible trap of living out of alignment with their truth.

I call it *Bossy Woo®*.

It's strategy meets soul. Intuition meets implementation. It's a way of doing life that blends divine guidance with real-world action. Sounds a little out there, right? Like your crystal-collecting cousin, and your spreadsheet-loving coworker teamed up to host a personal development retreat. But it works. Because you don't have to choose between being deeply spiritual and highly productive.

You get to be both.

Bossy Woo® is about tuning in to your intuition—and then doing something about it. It's clarity with a plan. Magic with a deadline. It's not sitting in a candlelit room waiting for answers. It's listening to the whisper *and* building the roadmap.

You might think, *Okay, but how do I know if I'm off track?*

Here's how: You feel stuck. Tired. Numb. Like life is happening around you, but not through you. You stand in the cereal aisle debating Raisin Bran vs. Cinnamon Toast Crunch, and somehow that moment becomes an existential crisis. You wonder how everyone else is out there thriving, glowing, building lives that light them up—while you're trying to remember if you paid that bill or replied to that email.

I've been there. I've lived that "stuckness."

From the outside, I was successful. But inside? I was running on autopilot. I knew there had to be more. And the moment I started listening to that knowing—that's when things shifted.

I believe that every single one of us has a purpose. Not just a job or title, but a soul-deep, divinely appointed reason for being here. It's not something you find on a mountaintop or in a five-year plan. It's already in you. It's been there the whole time.

You've seen it in the things that light you up. The moments when time disappears. When you forget to eat. When your whole body says, *Yes, this.* But we're taught to dismiss those things. To chase what's practical. To call our passions hobbies and our intuition nonsense.

But here's the truth:

Your joy is the map. Your intuition is the compass. And your purpose? That's the destination.

And when you follow that path—when you stop waiting for permission and start trusting your knowing—life opens up. Not instantly. Not effortlessly. But *honestly*. You begin to move with intention. You feel the difference between hustle and flow. You stop chasing someone else's version of success and start creating your own.

That's what happened to me.

And that's what I want for you.

Because this isn't just about being productive. It's about being *you*—fully, boldly, and on purpose.

You don't need another plan to follow. You need a reason to move. A vision to trust. A spark to say, *"Let's go."*

And that's where I come in.

So how do you go from "I feel stuck" to "Holy crap, I love my life"?

It starts with clarity.

So many high achievers wake up one day and feel like strangers to themselves. They've spent years building careers, chasing goals, collecting gold stars—but underneath it all, something's missing. And instead of asking what their soul actually wants, they reach for what's familiar: a new planner, a productivity hack, another degree.

But what they're really craving ... is purpose.

When you don't have clarity about why you're here, even success feels hollow. It's like driving a luxury car with no GPS—sure, you're moving, but do you even want to be where you're going?

That's why getting clear on your purpose matters.

Not just in a "let's journal about our dreams" kind of way. But in a real, grounded, *let's-figure-this-out* way. I walk people through exercises that help them connect the dots—between what excites them, what drains them, and what they're meant to do. And once they see it? It's like the fog lifts. Things start clicking. Energy returns. Confidence grows.

But clarity is just the beginning.

Next comes intuition.

Most people think of intuition as a bonus skill—something you tap into if you happen to be "that kind of person." But intuition isn't a luxury. It's a guidance system. It's how the Divine gets messages through the noise.

We all receive intuitive nudges differently. Some hear messages. Others feel physical sensations. Some people just *know* things out of nowhere. For me, it started with a weird tingling on my arms—like angel wings brushing my skin. Now, when I get chills? That's my signal. That's my "yes."

You have your own version of that. It might be subtle at first. But the more you pay attention, the louder it gets. The trick is learning your language. How does your intuition speak to you? That's where the real magic begins.

And let me be clear—you don't need to sit cross-legged on a mountaintop to hear it. You can tune in to your intuition while making dinner, driving to work, brushing your teeth. It's already there. You just have to *listen*.

But once you do? Once you start living in alignment with your purpose and intuition?

That's when stress tries to crash the party.

Let's be honest—most of us wear stress like a badge of honor. We bond over exhaustion. Brag about our packed calendars. Confuse burnout with ambition.

But stress isn't a productivity tool. It's a warning sign.

When you ignore stress, it messes with everything—your sleep, your creativity, your relationships. It keeps you reactive instead of intentional. And when you're making big life shifts? Stress will show up. Not because you're doing it wrong, but because you're stepping into something new.

So the question isn't "How do I avoid stress?" It's "How do I manage it in a way that supports my growth?"

That's where energy work comes in.

When your energy is blocked, even the best strategy won't land. You'll feel stuck. Tired. Disconnected. And no amount of productivity apps can fix that.

That's why I incorporate tools like Reiki, sound healing, and hypnosis—not to make things more complicated, but to help clear the static. These practices shift your nervous system. They get your energy flowing. They help you get out of your head and back into alignment.

Because when your energy is clear, your purpose becomes easier to follow. Your intuition becomes louder. Your decisions become lighter.

And once that happens? You're going to bump into something else.

Fear.

It's not loud at first. It sneaks in quietly. "Am I sure I can do this?" "What if I fail?" "Maybe just stay where it's safe."

Fear loves the comfort zone. It hates change. So every time you take a step toward alignment, fear tries to pull you back into familiar patterns.

But fear doesn't mean stop. It means *pay attention.*

The key isn't to fight it. It's to move through it.

I use tapping, hypnosis, and energy techniques to help people rewire the beliefs that keep them stuck. We don't pretend fear isn't real— we just stop letting it drive.

Because once fear loosens its grip?

Everything starts to shift.

The things that felt out of reach start to feel doable. The vision that once seemed too big starts to feel just right. You begin to trust that your dreams weren't random—they were assigned.

And now? You're finally ready to claim them.

This is the part where I could say, "Take your time. No rush."

But we both know that's not how transformation works.

The life you want? It's not waiting for you to feel "ready." It's waiting for you to say *yes.*

You don't need more permission. You don't need another sign. You don't need to check a few more boxes before you begin. If you're feeling that nudge—that pull—that whisper that says, *"It's time,"* that's not a coincidence.

That's your intuition talking.

And you can either keep silencing it, keep performing for an audience that doesn't even see the real you, keep showing up for a version of life that keeps you small—

Or you can decide.

To listen.

To trust.

To move.

Because the truth is, you weren't meant to live in survival mode. You weren't meant to build a life that looks good but feels empty. You weren't meant to stay stuck in a role that impresses others while disappointing your soul.

You were made for more.

You were made to be clear, confident, and connected. You were made to experience joy—not just in glimpses, but as a way of life. You were made to follow your intuition like a map, to use your voice with power, to claim your purpose like the gift it is.

That's what Bossy Woo® is all about.

It's not fluff. It's not fantasy. It's not about waiting for the universe to magically deliver your dream life with a bow on top.

It's about alignment. And action.

It's structure and spirit. It's deadlines and downloads. It's clarity and courage, and a big ol' "Let's do this!" energy that comes straight from your gut.

Because I'm not here to coddle you.

I'm here to remind you.

Of what you already know.

Of who you already are.

Of what's already waiting for you, if you're willing to take the next step.

So if you're standing on the edge of something big and wondering if it's the right time…

Let me just say it.

It is.

You are.

No more hiding. No more shrinking. No more waiting until things are perfect.

This is your moment.

Take a breath.

Consider yourself released.

You are free to go—free to choose, to create, to rise, to lead, to trust, to live.

And your time?

It starts now.

VALERIE HOLDEN

Valerie Holden is an intuitive life coach, author, and the visionary creator of Bossy Woo®—a transformational approach that helps women align with their true purpose. After more than 20 years as a police officer, Valerie traded in her badge for a new mission: guiding women through deep personal transformation. Blending grounded wisdom with spiritual insight, she helps her clients break free from what's holding them back so they can move forward with clarity, courage, and confidence.

www.ValerieHolden.com

WIRED FROM WITHIN: TRAIN THE MIND, UNLOCK THE MISSION, WIN FROM THE CORE

Sue Humphrey

I could start by telling you about the athletes I've coached to championships, or how I became the first person to receive the Nike Coach of the Year Award. I could talk about the Olympic Games—the medals, the records, the headlines.

But that's not where this story begins.

It starts with a nineteen-year-old girl who'd been kicked out of her house over a piercing—or maybe a tattoo. She was crashing on couches, failing out of school, and, by her own account, spiraling. At one point, she considered ending her life. She felt like a loser. She said so herself.

Then she found track and field.

She didn't come into the sport with technique or polish, but she had something you can't teach: raw talent. I saw it, and I invited her to train with me. What followed wasn't glamorous. It was hours of practice. Watching videos. Tweaking little things like her approach and takeoff. She worked hard, and I worked just as hard beside her.

Eventually, she started winning. First local meets, then bigger ones. She made the U.S. Olympic Team. But more importantly—she built a life. The sport gave her structure. Direction. She used to say I helped her learn how to "adult." That training with me taught her how to show up, stay consistent, and believe in herself.

And that's the part I care most about.

It's not just about winning. It's about the transformation. Helping someone go from feeling lost to finding their way. That's what coaching is. That's what keeps me doing this after all these years.

That's also why I care so much about coaching coaches. Because when you become a better coach, the ripple effects are enormous. You don't just change the results. You change lives.

Let me rewind a bit.

I was about fifteen—maybe fourteen—when I signed up for a high school class called audiovisual. Back then, that meant pushing around heavy projectors, so teachers could play movies. It was there that I met a girl two years older than me, who was one of the best sprinters in the country. She trained with college guys just to have someone who could keep up with her.

She invited me to practice. I went, watched, tried it myself—and quickly realized I was never going to be an elite athlete.

But I loved being part of it. So I became the team manager. I handled the stopwatch. Set up the starting blocks. I started reading library books about track and field. Learning everything I could. I was hooked.

When my sprinter friend left for college, I didn't want the journey to end. So her dad, my mom, and I started a girls' track team. I was sixteen and couldn't even drive myself to practice. We had no high school programs for girls back then. No scholarships. No real path forward.

But we made it work.

Then Title IX passed in the 1970s. Suddenly, schools began taking women's sports more seriously. I got a call from Arizona State. They offered me a part-time coaching role. I was also teaching elementary school full-time—because the coaching gig paid just $4,000 a year.

Still, I said yes.

Through the years, I've coached elite athletes and complete beginners. I've worked in Olympic stadiums and on dusty practice fields. But no matter where I've been, one thing has never changed: The real reward isn't the medal. It's the moment you see someone improve— really improve—and you know you helped make that happen.

So whether you're a coach, a parent, or just someone supporting a young athlete, I have one question for you: Are you giving them everything you've got?

Because they're giving everything they've got.

They're showing up, putting in the hours, working through fear, fatigue, and failure. Are you doing the same for them?

I'm not asking this to guilt you. I'm asking because you have more power than you think. When you grow, they grow. When you raise your standard, so do they. And when you learn how to support them better, they get better—on and off the field.

That's why I'm here. To share what I've learned, so you don't have to learn it the hard way.

Let's dive in.

Let's break this down—because greatness doesn't come from magic. It comes from mastery of the fundamentals.

For example, let's consider the long jump.

Sure, the crowd cheers for the flight. The airborne moment. The landing in the sand. But you and I know—the leap doesn't matter if the approach isn't solid. The magic in the air starts with what happens on the ground.

Every approach is a message: "I'm ready." But if that rhythm is off— even by a few inches—the whole jump crumbles. So what's our job as coaches? We don't just count steps. We help build trust—trust in the pattern, trust in the movement, trust in themselves.

Help your athletes find that rhythm. Help them feel it, not just measure it. Make it theirs. Make it consistent. Then do it again. And again. Until it's second nature.

Don't overlook the mental side. What they see in their mind becomes what they create with their body. When they can visualize themselves flying, they're halfway there. Confidence starts in the imagination.

Many times, we've practiced physical habits repeatedly. Yet, the real transfer of learning occurs when we release control and let our mind take over. We have confidence that the foundation is built. Now we go on "autopilot" and let the body execute the skills we've built. The mind can "trick" the body into believing they are performing. When this happens, amazing performances are seen.

And all of that?

It starts with the basics. The foundation. The boring stuff that nobody claps for, but everybody needs. That's where champions are built—not in the highlight, but in the hidden work.

So when you're coaching—don't just focus on the form. Focus on the fire. The why behind the movement. Because if you can help an athlete believe in their approach, their lift, their arc ... you're not just coaching technique.

Your coaching courage.

This is a piece a lot of coaches overlook. We get so focused on form, drills, and results that we forget we're coaching people—not just performances.

Learning something new is hard. It's humbling. And for many young athletes, it makes them feel vulnerable. They don't want to mess up in front of you—or their teammates. If you're not actively encouraging them, you're missing one of your most powerful coaching tools.

Some kids will get it right away. Others will take weeks. That doesn't mean they're not trying—it just means their path is different. And it's your job to meet them there.

I once coached a jumper who couldn't seem to stop fouling the jump by going over the takeoff mark. Week after week, same mistake. But we kept working. Kept watching video. Kept tweaking. And then— one day—it clicked. That athlete became one of the best jumpers in the nation.

If I'd given up too early, we would've missed it.

So be patient. Keep encouraging. Let them fail safely—and help them build confidence from that failure.

Finally, you will piece everything together for that awesome performance.

If you're serious about helping your athletes succeed, you can't just wing it. You need a structured plan. One that's built around clear goals, gradual progression, and realistic timelines.

A good program starts with what you want to achieve: Speed? Strength? Power? Choose a focus. Then map out the drills, routines, and rest days that will support that goal.

Rest isn't a luxury—it's part of the plan. Many times, mental and emotional rest is more important than physical recovery.

Track progress. Keep notes. Reassess every few weeks. A successful program is flexible. It evolves with your athlete.

When you create structure, you create safety. And when an athlete feels safe and supported, they push harder. They trust more. They grow faster.

That's when the actual results show up.

*   *   *

In 1996, I had the privilege of coaching Charles Austin in the high jump at the Olympic Games in Atlanta.

We'd worked together for six years. Drills. Film. Adjustments. Encouragement. All of it, over and over again. He wasn't just chasing a medal—he was mastering his craft. We both were.

Right before the final, as Charles boarded the athlete bus, he turned to me and said, "Time to go to work." My response was, "Have fun!"

That calm confidence? It didn't come from luck. It came from preparation.

He won gold that day. But what stayed with me wasn't just the win—it was what I learned. That we can control how we prepare, how we train, how we show up. But once the moment arrives, we must let go and trust we've done enough.

That lesson applies to all of us. Whether you're coaching Olympians or kids at a weekend meet, your job is the same: Prepare them well, believe in them deeply, and let the results follow.

You won't always know what they'll become. You won't always see the end of the story. Maybe they'll make it to college. Maybe they won't. Maybe they'll win state. Maybe they'll just fall in love with a sport that teaches them how to believe in themselves. Maybe they'll love themselves and the person you have helped them become.

But none of that happens without you.

You don't have to be perfect. But you do have to be committed.

Committed to showing up. Committed to learning. Committed to giving them your best, so they can discover theirs.

I've been coaching since I was a teenager. I've stood at the top of the sport. And still—every day—I'm learning. I'm refining. I'm getting better.

Because the athletes I coach? They're doing the same.

So, let me ask you one more time: Are you?

Are you giving these kids everything you've got?

Because if you are—then I'm with you. Every step of the way. Let's go to work. Let's have fun!

SUE HUMPHREY

Before Sue Humphrey coached an Olympic champion, she started coaching track & field with a group of elementary school girls on a dusty field in Phoenix, AZ—back when girls didn't even have school teams. Title IX changed that.

Arizona State University came calling, and her coaching journey took flight—from Arizona State to Long Beach State to The University of Texas, and eventually to three Olympic Games. She led the U.S. Women's Olympic Track & Field Team in 2004 and coached the first woman to ever high jump over 2 meters indoors.

Today, with 50+ years under her belt, Coach Sue is still on the track and in the field, shaping champions at Phoenix high schools.

www.SueHumphreyCoach.com

FREEDOM HAS A VOICE: THE ASTOUNDING IMPACT OF SPEAKING THE TRUTH

Gaby Jordan

How free do you want to be?

Consider that question—not as a nice idea, but as a real invitation. Not how successful do you want to be. Not how productive, or admired, or balanced. But: how free?

That question showed up one afternoon when I got into the subway to see my ex-husband. Sixteen years had passed since we ended our marriage. We had moved on. We had both built full, happy lives. Children. New relationships. New careers. From the outside, everything was great. But something in me was still carrying weight. Something unspoken had never been said.

It wasn't about closure. It wasn't about drama. It wasn't about some emotional mixtape I'd saved for just such a moment. It was about truth.

There was a conversation I hadn't had. And I couldn't move forward—fully, freely—until I had it.

The topic isn't important—but you are going to wonder the whole time—so I should tell you. It was that I'd cheated on him. A few times. And while we had long since untangled our lives, I had never owned that part of the story with him. Not directly. Not aloud.

You'd think someone like me—someone who helps others communicate, grow, evolve—would have had that conversation already. But like so many of us, I had tucked it away, told myself it didn't matter anymore. I told myself that by that time, it was old news, in the past, no need to deal with it.

But time doesn't heal what you're still hiding from. Time just makes it quieter.

I didn't want to bring up the past to relive it. In fact, I didn't really even want to say it. But I did want to speak it, so I could finally set it down. I wanted to stop rehearsing the guilt in my own mind, and instead release it into the open air—where it might just dissolve in the light of day.

So I called him.

"Can we talk?" I asked.

And what happened next surprised us both.

It wasn't the details that mattered. It wasn't a rehashing of pain or betrayal. It was that, for the first time, everything was said. Nothing left between us. No invisible thread tugging at the fabric of the present. Just truth. Just presence.

And in that space, something unexpected happened.

We became more connected than ever.

Not out of nostalgia, or pity, or some Hollywood-style reconciliation. We became connected because the story between us was no longer holding either of us hostage. We were both free.

In fact, I became his coach. Yes—his coach. I've coached my ex-husband through conversations with various people in his life— notably his next ex-wife and new love interests.

At one point, I remember thinking, *Is this what healing looks like? Or am I starring in a Hallmark fantasy?*

But that's what happens when you have a conversation that matters. You make space for what's next.

The truth is most of us are walking around with unresolved things. Unspoken words. Unshared truths. Tiny threads of guilt or regret that quietly hum in the background of our lives. And those threads tug at more than our hearts. They tug at our leadership. Our creativity. Our relationships. Our results.

That voice in your head—the one that whispers, "You're not ready," or "You don't deserve it," or "You're not whole"—it's not just your inner critic. It's incongruence. It's the part of you that knows what's true and feels the cost of not saying it.

We think those things live in the past. But they live in our nervous systems. Our choices. Our silence.

It actually costs us—

All of that is EXPENSIVE.* And not just financially.

And here's the part that matters most: You can't access your full power when part of you is still holding back.

So how do we move forward?

We talk.

But not just any kind of talk. We have what I call **champion conversations**—the kind that create clarity, peace, and forward motion. The kind that aren't about being right or getting closure, but about reclaiming freedom.

And yes, there's a way to do this that doesn't require burning bridges or turning every interaction into a therapy session.

It starts simply.

Write it down.

Whatever "it" is—the thing you need to say, the thing you're afraid of, the story you keep replaying—start there. Get it out of your head and onto the page. Do a brain dump if you have to—let it all out. That begins the process.

Then **organize your thoughts** (*on paper*) in preparation for the conversation.

Why is this conversation important? Why has it been hard? What are you afraid will happen if you finally speak (and actually say it)?

The act of writing—or speaking—uncorks the energy. It begins the process of congruence.

Then **take responsibility**.

Not for everything. Just for your part.

Maybe you were silent when something felt wrong. Maybe you didn't express a boundary or left something unsaid because it felt easier in the moment. Responsibility is not about blame—it's about reclaiming your integrity. It's about saying, "This is how I contributed, and I'm ready to do something different now."

And then, **speak from your truth**—not *the* truth.

Let go of proving, defending, accusing. Use "I" statements. Say what's real for you. "I felt invisible when that happened." "Here's the meaning I made of it."

Not, "You always do this" or "You never cared."

This is not about winning. This is about resolving.

Next, **listen. Really listen.**

Not to prep your counterpoint. Not to validate your feelings. Just to understand them. Ask, "What did you hear me say?" or "What is your reaction to what I said?" And when they answer, reflect it back. Say, "Let me make sure I got that."

Because here's the thing: People don't need you to agree with them. They need to feel heard.

And finally—one of the most important parts and what people avoid--**create agreements** for what comes next.

This is where most people stop. They say the hard thing. They cry. They exhale. They say, "Phew, glad that's over."

But that's only part of it.

Without a new agreement, nothing changes. And then, when the same thing happens again, we say, "See? That didn't work." But it's not that the conversation failed—we didn't prepare for the future. People don't change that fast, so don't be surprised if they (or you) make a mistake in the future—just plan for how you will deal with it if it comes about again.

A new agreement might be small: "Check in with me if I go quiet." Or "Let's pause before things escalate." Or even, "Next time, let's not talk about life over sandwiches."

It doesn't need to be dramatic. It just needs to be *real*.

This is the real work of growth. Not the lightning-bolt moment. Not the viral quote or the perfectly worded apology. The real work is choosing to be congruent—over and over again. Even when it's uncomfortable. Especially when it is.

Because here's what I've seen, over and over, in my work with leaders, entrepreneurs, creatives, parents, and partners: The thing you think is holding you back? The pattern you can't seem to break? The result that never quite lands?

It's not because you're lazy. Or broken. Or missing some magical strategy.

It's because there's a conversation that hasn't been had.

One that's sitting just below the surface of your story, quietly influencing your confidence, your choices, your next move.

And it doesn't need to be loud or dramatic. It just needs to be said.

Because when you speak what's true—even gently, even privately— you begin to reclaim your life.

I've coached people who've spent years climbing ladders, only to realize they were standing on unfulfilling ground. People who've built empires on top of silenced pain. People who've led entire teams while quietly holding their breath, afraid someone might discover the unresolved story running beneath it all.

But when they tell the truth? When they have that conversation.

Not for closure. Not for revenge. Not because their therapist said to. But for freedom.

Everything begins to shift.

Because you can't create something new from a place that's hiding. You can't lead when your own voice is muffled. You can't grow if you're still rehearsing guilt in the shadows.

So again, I'll ask you: How free do you want to be? Let that question sit on your heart. Let it move through the stuck places. Let it tap you on the shoulder in quiet moments. Because it's not just a question. It's a compass.

It points to the part of your life where something still feels unfinished. It points to the words you haven't yet said. It points to the truth that's waiting—not to explode, but to be integrated.

You are not here to be perfect. You're here to be whole. And wholeness doesn't come from pretending nothing ever happened. It comes from daring to face what did—and speaking it, with care and courage.

Your life is shaped by your actions. Your actions are driven by your feelings. Your feelings are formed by your thoughts. And your thoughts—many of them—were shaped in the dark, by things you never named, patterns you never questioned, stories you never voiced.

But when you bring them into the light? When you speak with intention, love, and truth?

You make space for something new. Not just in your relationships, but in your nervous system. Your creativity. Your leadership. Your peace.

And that is the gift of a champion conversation. It doesn't fix the past. It frees you from it. So if there's a conversation you haven't had—one that's been quietly waiting, whispering in the background of your life—maybe now is the time.

Not for drama. Not for closure. But for freedom.

And maybe, just maybe, what waits on the other side isn't loss, judgment or conflict. Maybe what waits is more than you imagined:

Peace. Clarity. Connection. Forward motion. Maybe what waits is *you*—the unburdened, untangled, fully expressed version of you.

So again, I'll ask one last time: How free do you want to be?

And are you willing to say what needs to be said ... to become who you already are?

Footnote:

*$62.4 million per year: The average cost of poor communication to companies with 100,000+ employees.
—*SHRM & Holmes Report*

Every avoided conversation costs an average of $7,500 and more than seven work days.
—*Crucial Conversations / VitalSmarts*

70 percent of employees avoid difficult conversations with their boss, coworkers, or direct reports.
— *Bravely / Harris Poll*

One in five employees report that avoiding conflict has caused them to quit a job.
— *Bravely*

GABY JORDAN

Gaby Jordan, CEO of Source Elements Group and Founder of Human Better EDU, is dedicated to empowering executives and teams to achieve exponential results through aligned cultures. With over 25 years of experience, she has coached leaders in major companies and led educational programs in over 80 institutions, including MIT and Stanford. Her passion for education stems from her own journey, being the first in her family to attend college and law school. Gaby's unique approach brings transformative tools to both the corporate world and education, fostering responsible community members. She lives in NYC with her husband, where they enjoy making music together.

www.SourceElementsGroup.com

HORMONE REBELLION: WHY PLAYING NICE WITH AGING IS KILLING YOUR ENERGY

Julie Kaanapu, NBC-HWC

Have you ever had your smoke detector go off when you're just trying to make toast? The noise is shrill. You're waving towels, hitting buttons, shouting at plastic. And all the while, what if the real fire is actually downstairs, growing in the basement?

Now imagine this: You call the fire department, and instead of putting out the fire, they just take the batteries out of the smoke detector.

"There. No more noise. You're fine."

Sounds absurd, right?

But that's exactly what happens every time a woman walks into a doctor's office, saying, "I don't feel right," and hears, "Your labs look normal."

Oh really? Then why do I feel like a half-deflated pool float abandoned in the yard?

Here's the truth: "Normal" isn't the same as "healthy," and it's definitely not the same as "optimal." You know your body. You know when something's off. But the system is built to treat numbers on a chart—not the real, messy, human experience of a woman who is

173

exhausted, foggy, anxious, irritable, and wondering where the hell her spark went.

I've seen it too many times. A woman walks in with symptoms like no energy, low libido, mood swings, stubborn belly fat—and she walks out with a prescription and a pat on the back.

No answers. No support. Just more confusion and a creeping sense of hopelessness.

I call it F.L.A.B.B.—Fatigue, Low Libido, Anxiety, Brain Fog, Belly Fat. And if you've experienced it, you know exactly how real and disruptive it can be.

But here's the thing: these symptoms aren't "just aging." They're signals. Smoke alarms. And we've been trained to silence them instead of putting out the fire.

When your hormones are optimized—your life is energized. That's not just a catchy phrase. That's the reality I help women reclaim every single day.

You know that twenty-something energy you used to have? When you could eat pizza at 2 a.m. and still show up for work the next morning? That wasn't just youth—it was peak hormones. And as those hormones decline, which can start in our late twenties, everything changes.

But most doctors? They don't talk about that. They don't test for it. Or worse, they don't understand how to treat it, other than prescribing medications with side effects.

That's where I come in.

With decades of experience in health—from sports medicine to hormone optimization—I've made it my mission to help women stop settling for "fine" and start feeling phenomenal.

Because tired isn't normal. Brain fog isn't inevitable. And living in a body that feels foreign and disconnected? That's not just part of getting older.

There is another way. And you don't have to go it alone.

*   *   *

Let's start by getting one thing straight: Not all hormones are the same.

Your body runs on a delicate balance of them—testosterone, estrogen, progesterone, thyroid, DHEA, and more. These aren't extras. They're essential. When even one of them is off, everything starts to feel off.

So when you forget things, wake up exhausted, drag through your day, snap at your family, and feel like a foggy, irritable stranger in your own body—that's not "just aging." That's your body trying to get your attention.

But the typical response? Here's a statin. Here's a sleep aid. Here's something for your anxiety.

And suddenly, your medicine cabinet is overflowing—but you still feel like crap.

The problem isn't you. The problem is the system.

According to *The New York Times*, when residency programs were surveyed across internal medicine, family medicine and gynecology residents, they included maybe one or two total hours of education about menopause. About 20 percent of residents said they'd had no menopause education.

So when they look at your labs and tell you you're "normal," what they really mean is, "I don't know how to help you beyond this."

And let's be honest: "Normal" isn't working for most people. Lab ranges are based on the average population—not on what it means to feel *great*. So if everyone else is tired, inflamed, and foggy … guess what "normal" looks like?

But you don't want normal. You want optimal. You want to feel like yourself again—or maybe better than you ever have.

Now let's talk about nutrition and nutraceuticals—vitamins, minerals, and nutrients your body needs but doesn't make on its own. Once upon a time, we got these through food. But today's soil is depleted, our food is processed, and you'd need twelve bowls of spinach to get the same iron nutrients your grandmother got in one.

That's why targeted supplementation matters. Not guesswork—testing. Because if you're deficient in vitamin D, B vitamins, or lack proper gut flora (to name just a few), no amount of willpower will fix your fatigue. Your body isn't broken. It's running on empty.

And then there's quality. Not all supplements are created equal. Some store-bought options are contaminated or so poorly absorbed they do more harm than good. You deserve better than that. You deserve support that's based on science, not shelf space.

The same goes for hormones. Bioidentical hormones—those that match your body's natural chemistry—can make a night-and-day difference. But many women are handed synthetic versions that don't communicate properly with their cells. It's like putting diesel in a car that runs on unleaded. Sure, it runs … but not well.

When hormones are optimized correctly, things begin to shift.

You start sleeping through the night. Your moods even out. The belly fat starts to budge. You remember things. You want sex again. You feel *awake*.

And when you finally find a provider who gets it? It's life-changing.

But not everyone will understand. You might go back to your regular doctor, glowing with energy, and they'll say, "What are you doing? That's dangerous!"

You'll be caught between a system that fears change and a new reality that finally feels right. But the sad thing is that eighty years of literature has shown the safety and benefits of bioidentical hormone optimization. This isn't anything new. It's only new to those who have ignored and feared it.

And if you let fear win? You'll slide back into fatigue, fog, and frustration.

That's why I've spent over a decade training doctors and clinics on preventative medicine and hormone optimization. Because this shouldn't be revolutionary. It should be standard care.

But until it is, you have to be your own advocate.

Ask the right questions. Understand your labs. Challenge "normal." Choose providers who see the whole you, not just your numbers.

You're not crazy. You're not lazy. And you're not broken.

You're just ready for a new kind of care.

*   *   *

I know what you might be thinking.

"I've tried everything."
"I'm too far gone."
"What if this doesn't work for me?"

Let me gently push back and say: It's not about trying everything—it's about trying what actually works. Not random diets, not quick-fix cleanses, not prescriptions that patch over symptoms. What works is understanding your body, supporting it properly, and reclaiming the energy that was *always* meant to be yours.

Because the truth is, this isn't just about hormones. It's about power. Your power.

Every time you choose to advocate for yourself, to say, "This isn't good enough," to challenge a broken system—you are taking your power back. You're saying yes to living, not just surviving. Yes to energy, focus, passion, purpose.

And you're not doing it just for you.

When one woman rises, she lights the way for others. Her daughters see it. Her friends feel it. Her doctor notices it. She changes the conversation—because she refused to stay quiet in the face of "You're fine."

This is your moment.

To stop settling.
To stop silencing the alarm.
To stop apologizing for wanting to feel good.

Because you deserve to feel amazing in your body. You deserve to wake up excited about your day. You deserve to live the second half of your life with more fire than the first.

And I'll say it one more time—because it's the heart of everything I do:

When your hormones are optimized, your life is energized.

Let's make that your new normal.

JULIE KAANAPU

Julie Kaanapu, NBC-HWC has over 25 years in the health industry, passionate about coaching clients to achieve their health goals and consulting physicians on hormone optimization and preventative medicine to improve patient outcomes and reduce risk of disease.

She has a duel bachelor's degree in sports medicine & biology from the University of Oregon, is a national board-certified health & wellness coach, certified in functional nutrition, certified life coach, certified graduate of Worldlink Medical, a physician liaison, medical consultant & trainer with Biote Medical, a speaker, leadership coach, and author.

Her passion is to educate and empower women over 40 who feel overlooked by the medical system and struggle with symptoms of F.L.A.B.B. (fatigue, low libido, anxiety, brain fog & belly fat), how to take control of their health, and optimize their quality of life without unnecessary medications!

www.ProHealthShare.com

MONEY DOESN'T FOLLOW CHAOS: WHAT ELSE MAKES STRATEGIC LEADERS WIN

Rachel Kaberon

Let's just call it: A lot of us are running our businesses like Goldilocks.

Wandering into new territory, we use familiar signposts to navigate and come to expect that things we didn't build—and didn't create—will somehow lead us to feeling "just right." It's clever. It's scrappy. But it's not leadership. It's improvisation in someone else's living room.

Goldilocks didn't have a plan. She had great instincts, curiosity, and a talent for disrupting existing order—breaking metaphorical chairs and sampling whatever looked appealing. Sound familiar?

You're talented. Driven. Drawn to adventure. Lured by the mystery of what's possible without fully understanding risk and its nature. Maybe your daring pulls you toward the roller coaster, where you mistake the thrilling experience of a closed loop for the real challenge of managing uncertainty and change.

It's great to be wide-eyed, enthusiastic, and eager to capture the golden opportunities in sight. But leaning into what we know is make-believe—just like believing that more productivity will automatically advance growth, or that adding processes will magically yield progress.

Caught up in a swirl of high-stakes demands that turn our calendars into Jenga towers, we limit our flexibility and settle for the illusion of stability and balance.

You've got the ambition. You've got the drive. But traction? That's what's missing.

And people keep telling you to "be patient" or "trust the process." Meanwhile, your bank account is dwindling and you're scrambling for scraps.

Here's what no one's saying loudly enough: You are not the problem.

The problem is glare and noise—doing too much of the right-*looking* stuff with too little clarity.

You don't need another productivity app, or a pep talk from someone who learned business by watching YouTube ads in a Lamborghini. You need strategy. You need direction. You need to lead—not react.

Because here's the deal: Money doesn't follow chaos. It doesn't reward exhaustion. It doesn't throw itself at hustle.

Money loves leadership.

And leadership without strategy? That's just Goldilocks with a business license and a motivational podcast.

You want to stop spinning your wheels? Start making decisions based on clear vision—not your mood.

Beyond the Porridge Test

That's where I come in. I help leaders—founders, creatives, scrappy teams, "I've-got-five-tabs-open-in-my-brain" types—find clarity in the chaos.

Not by shouting louder, but by listening deeper. Not by doing more, but by doing what matters. With intention. With curiosity. With strategy.

You can't pitch your way to traction if your message isn't landing. You can't lead if your team is still trying to figure out where the story begins.

Leadership starts with vision. With story. With the ability to set the scene so that your people—your team, your clients, your audience—actually know where they're going and why it matters.

If you don't set that scene? Everyone stands around holding their props, waiting for direction.

You've got to give them the script—and not just any script, one that actually fits the world you're trying to build. Because otherwise, they'll just keep defaulting to the old one.

Unlike Goldilocks, who simply tested what was already there, real leaders create the conditions that feel "just right" for everyone involved.

Strategy That Actually Works

Let's start with strategy.

Not the buzzword version. Not "what's your North Star?" scribbled on a sticky note. I'm talking about real, flexible, vision-backed strategy that gives your activities direction—especially when things get weird. Because they will.

Strategy is not your tagline. It's not your elevator pitch. It's the framework that holds you steady when your launch tanks, your team burns out, and your motivation gets buried under too many emails, stretched across three Slack channels, and fueled by a half-eaten protein bar.

Think of it like this: Strategy is the difference between a chessboard and a dartboard. One is deliberate, with each move building toward a larger purpose. The other is just hoping something sticks.

Now, let's talk about stretching into that forward-thinking, strategic mindset—what I call *framestretching*.

It's not about being flexible in the yoga-retreat sense. It's about shifting your mental lens when everything feels stuck. It's about asking different questions. Instead of "What's wrong with me?" ask, "What else could be true?"

"What else?" is my favorite question in the world. It's deceptively simple and wildly effective. Because the first answer people give you? That's usually the rehearsed one. The safe one. But "what else?" is where the truth lives. That's where you find values, fears, and unspoken expectations hiding under the surface.

When you start asking that in your business, you stop assuming what your people need—and start learning.

That's strategy in motion. That's how leaders think.

Leadership Without the Throne

Now—leadership.

It's not the loudest person in the Zoom room. It's not charisma or job titles, or being the one who organizes the color-coded slide deck. It's accountability. Vision. Forward motion.

Real leaders say, "If this succeeds—I'm in. If this flops—I'm still in."

They bring people with them, not just because they're inspiring, but because they're *clear*.

You don't have to be perfect. You have to be present.

You have to decide what matters, focus the energy, and keep moving—even if you're duct-taping things together as you go.

The beautiful part? Leadership doesn't have to be lonely. It can be collaborative. Dynamic. Human.

But someone has to say, "Let's go."

Someone has to mean it.

Process as Your Secret Weapon

Which brings us to something most people love to hate: *process.*

Yes, I said it.

Process gets a bad rap because it sounds rigid. But in truth? Process is what keeps creativity from combusting.

When process is working, you're free to innovate, explore, and lead. When it breaks? You're stuck in the self-checkout-meltdown version of your business—everything's beeping, no one knows what to do, and someone's calling for a manager.

Process isn't bureaucracy—it's a time-saving, risk-managing, stress-reducing sanity device. It turns chaos into momentum.

The real magic of process? Once it becomes second nature, you don't have to think about it. You just *do it*—freeing up mental energy to think, dream, and lead.

The Power of Clear Storytelling

Finally, let's talk about the heart of everything: *storytelling.*

Because if people don't understand what you do, they won't trust you. And if they don't trust you, they won't follow you.

Forget jargon. Forget the forty-seven-slide pitch deck. Tell a story. Preferably, one almost as simple as Goldilocks—but with better outcomes for everyone involved.

Stories clarify. They connect. They humanize.

In a world full of noise, a clear story is a power move.

You don't have to be a novelist. Just be real. Explain what's at stake. Who's involved. What changed. Why it matters.

That's what makes strategy digestible.

That's what makes leadership feel possible.

And that's what turns ideas into action.

Because at the end of the day, no one follows data. They follow meaning.

Time to Leave the Woods

Let's land this.

Not with a recap. Not with a checklist. Just a moment of truth.

You don't need to do it all today. You don't need to master the art of strategy overnight or walk into your next meeting with a color-coded map of the future.

But you *do* need to begin.

Option 1: Recently, I worked with a CEO who decided it was time to scale up. She had a brilliant idea, but zero experience forging strategic partnerships or attracting serious capital. Like Goldilocks, she'd been wandering into unfamiliar territory, using whatever felt familiar to navigate, but nothing felt "just right" anymore. She was well past her comfort zone.

When we sat down to explore her indecision and sort through her assumptions, we knew she needed more than instinct. So we examined parallels in alternative industries, asking, "What else?" until she began to see that something different was possible.

It paid off. Not only did she land a meeting with an ideal partner, but our prep work refocused that call on the value they actually needed. She walked away with her first significant investor, not because she'd found the perfect-temperature porridge, but because she'd learned to set the table herself.

Option 2: There's an ancient principle that says: "It is not your duty to complete the work, but neither are you free to desist from it." You're not responsible for fixing everything, but you don't get to check out either. You're here to lead—not flawlessly, but strategically.

Option 3: The difference between you and Goldilocks? She left the bears' house not exactly as she found it—broken chairs, rumpled beds, chaos in her wake. You have the opportunity to build something better, to create the conditions where "just right" isn't an accident, but a deliberate choice.

You've got the instincts. You've got the insight. Now give them direction.

Stop waiting for perfect conditions, official permission, or a round of applause. Start where you are. Set the scene. Ask better questions. Be the one who leads—not with noise, but with clarity.

Because money isn't falling in love with the loudest person in the room. It's watching for the one who's got a plan—and the guts to follow it through.

You don't need to reinvent the wheel.

But what if the next breakthrough, the next idea that shifts everything, has your name on it?

It's not waiting.

Let's go.

RACHEL KABERON

Rachel Kaberon helps leaders find clarity in chaos. As a strategic advisor and framestretching coach, she works with founders, creative teams, and "five-tabs-open-in-my-brain" executives who have the drive but need the direction. Rachel specializes in turning ambitious ideas into actionable strategies through her signature "what else?" methodology. When she's not helping CEOs, and founder teams navigate uncharted territory, she's probably asking better questions, setting clearer scenes, and proving that money really does love leadership. Her work has helped clients secure significant partnerships, attract serious capital, and build businesses that feel as good as they perform.

www.FrameStretching.com

YOUR 'ONE WORD' IDENTITY: CLEARLY COMMUNICATE WHO YOU ARE AND CREATE UNSTOPPABLE OPPORTUNITIES!

Rich Keller, The CATALYST

Let's do a little thought experiment.

Picture three brands: Apple. Snickers. Taylor Swift.

Now, without overthinking it—what's the very first word that pops into your head for each?

It doesn't have to be clever or correct. Just instinctual.

Chances are, your first thought was what they are: a phone, a candy bar, a singer. But that's not branding. Branding isn't what something is. It's about the benefit. When done right, it speaks volumes in an instant.

Now imagine this:

What if *you* could do the same thing?

What if someone said, "Tell me about yourself," and instead of fumbling through your job title, past experiences, or list of credentials … you answered with one word.

Not a catchphrase. Not a humblebrag. Just a single, powerful word that defined you at your core.

That's the power of personal branding.

That's the magic of discovering your *One Word*.

Because we've all been there—standing in an interview, on a stage, or in a networking conversation—and we get hit with the four words that make people simultaneously sit up and shrink back:

"Tell me about yourself."

It sounds simple, even conversational. But it throws people off every time. The mind races. "Where do I begin?" becomes the default internal panic. We start grabbing at titles, roles, anything that might explain who we are.

But here's the truth: people don't want a resume. They want a *connection*.

And in today's world, where everyone's competing for attention, the way you stand out isn't by shouting louder—it's by speaking clearer. Simpler. Truer.

That's what your *One Word* gives you.

It unlocks your story. It gives people a reason to remember you. It bridges the gap between what you *do* and who you *are*.

I know this because I lived the opposite for years.

For most of my adult life, I defined myself by external labels. I was a dad. A marathoner. A cancer survivor. A marketer.

Each of those was part of my life, but none of them captured the core of my identity.

Then one day, in a job interview, a recruiter looked me in the eye and said: "Rich, I can't hire you. We need someone who will maintain the brand as-is. But you're not that guy. You're a *catalyst*. You shake things up."

At the time, it stung. I felt rejected. But later, I realized—she wasn't rejecting me; she was *branding* me.

That One Word—Catalyst—became the mirror I didn't know I needed. It helped me see that my value wasn't in preserving what was; it was in sparking what could be.

And the irony? That recruiter did for me what I had done for companies for over twenty-five years.

As a brand marketer, I worked with some of the most iconic names in the world: Oreo, Planters, Godiva, Chips Ahoy! I didn't just market products—I helped shape emotional identities.

Over the course of my career, I developed what I now call my One Word Philosophy. It's rooted in three beliefs:

First, a brand is more than a logo or a tagline. It's an *emotional identity* that tells people how it improves their life.

Second, at the heart of every brand is one *defining quality*—its Core Value.

And third, that Core Value can be distilled into a single, powerful word.

So I asked myself: If this works for billion-dollar brands, could it work for people, too?

What if people could distill their identity down to a Core Value—and use that to shape how they show up in the world?

And more importantly, what happens *after* they do?

Let's go back to those three brands for a moment: Apple. Snickers. Taylor Swift.

When I ask audiences to tell me their first associations with those brands, most say things like:

Apple? "MacBook" or "iPhone."
Snickers? "Candy bar" or "chocolate."
Taylor Swift? "Pop star" or "Swiftie."

That's natural—but it's surface-level. They're describing the *category*, not the *Core Value*. But when we look deeper, here's what emerges:

Apple creates simplicity.

Snickers delivers *satisfaction*.
Taylor Swift is a *storyteller*.

That's what people *really* buy. Not the product—the core value behind the product.

And the same applies to you. People aren't connecting with your job title or credentials. They're connecting with *your* Core Value.

That's what personal branding is: communicating the value you bring to others. It's not about performance—it's about impact. About knowing who you are and how you improve the lives around you.

And here's the good news: You already have that core value. You just need to name it. When you discover your One Word, it brings two forms of powerful clarity.

First, **clarity for others.**

Your One Word becomes the thread that ties your story together. It gives people a clear, cohesive picture of who you are and how you've made a difference. It creates resonance. Recognition. Connection.

It helps people remember you—not because you impressed them, but because you *mattered* to them.

Second, **clarity for yourself.**

Your One Word becomes your compass. It guides your choices. It helps you say yes to the right opportunities—and no to the wrong ones. It aligns your work, your relationships, your goals with who you are at your core.

It's the difference between drifting and *directing* your life.

I call it the Eureka Moment, that point when everything clicks—your past makes sense, your present feels aligned, and your future opens up with confidence.

That's what I want for you.

Because whether you're a business leader, an entrepreneur, a student, or someone in transition, the challenge is the same:

You're trying to cut through the noise. You're trying to be seen. You're trying to move forward with clarity, and One Word can do all that—if it meets three criteria:

It has to be **believable.** It must reflect who you truly are—not who you think others want you to be.

It needs to be **simple.** One word. No jargon. No overexplaining.

It should be **memorable.** Something that sticks in people's minds and leaves a lasting impression.

Because that's what great brands do—and you are no different.

You are a brand. You carry a message, and your One Word is how you deliver it to the world.

So the next time someone asks, "Tell me about yourself," you won't need a script. You won't panic. You won't hide behind titles or timelines. You'll smile. You'll stand tall, and you'll speak with clarity.

Because you'll know exactly who you are—and what you bring to the world to make it better. That's what this journey is about. We spend so much time perfecting what we do, but so little time asking who we are. Maybe it's time we change that.

My One Word—*Catalyst*—has completely reshaped my life. It's given me the clarity to leave behind a career that no longer fits and the courage to step into my true calling.

Now, I help others discover theirs. Because clarity creates confidence, and confidence leads to action. It doesn't take a full rebrand. It doesn't take a life overhaul. It just takes One Word.

And your One Word … can change everything.

RICH KELLER

Rich Keller has leveraged his One Word philosophy to shape iconic brand identities at Nabisco, Kraft, Cadbury, and Godiva. After discovering his own One Word, CATALYST, he left his corporate career to pursue his mission of transforming 1M lives, One Word at a time. A TEDx speaker and Wharton MBA, Rich now focuses on Personal Branding, helping individuals uncover their core value, authentically express who they are, and build a unique identity that guides their life and career with purpose. He lives in New Jersey with his wife and two children. Fun fact: he owns 50 Buffs, his signature headgear.

www.TheRichKeller.com

FROM INVISIBLE TO INVINCIBLE: FIVE PRECISION MOVES TO WIN AT WORK

Alexis King, MBA

"I am not going to be ignored."

If that line immediately triggered the image of a frizzy-haired Glenn Close staring down Michael Douglas in *Fatal Attraction*, then you and I are already speaking the same language.

Now don't worry, I'm not encouraging you to channel that exact level of intensity at work. I'm not suggesting you start stalking your HR director or harm animals in any way.

But what I *am* saying is … maybe Glenn had a point.

Because in your career, the people who get ahead, the ones who land the best jobs, snag the promotions, and have leadership circling their names in meetings, aren't always the ones who work the hardest. They're the ones who refuse to be overlooked.

Let that sink in for a minute.

If you're a mid-career professional who's been grinding for years by staying late, raising your hand, running on caffeine, and waiting for someone to finally recognize your worth … it's time to face the truth.

They won't. Truly, they will not, and I understand any frustration around that.

You will not get their attention and recognition, unless you change the rules of the game.

You see, most of us were taught that hard work is the path to success. If we do more, give more, answer emails at midnight, and volunteer for every project, someone will eventually reward our effort.

But here's the thing: Hard work alone doesn't make you visible. It makes you dependable. It makes you efficient. Mostly, it makes you invisible, and often, it leads to extreme frustration.

So you need a different strategy.

You need to become unignorable, so they see you as invincible.

Now, I know that word might sound aggressive, but I want you to think about it like this: Being unignorable doesn't mean being loud, pushy, or political. Being invincible means showing up in such a powerful, clear, strategic way that when the big opportunities arise, your name is already on the list.

That's where **The Career Ninja Mindset™** comes in.

Ninjas don't stumble into success. They study. They adapt. They move with precision. They don't rely on brute force—they master their timing. They're effective, strategic, and most of all, intentional.

And that's what you need to be to become unignorable, because let me tell you, while you're waiting to feel "ready," some guy named Chad, with half your qualifications and twice your confidence, is already applying. He sees a job listing with seven requirements, checks off three, and says, "Close enough." Meanwhile, you're checking off six and convincing yourself you need a certification before you can hit submit.

I'm not saying we all need to be Chad, but we do need to change the way we evaluate ourselves.

You don't need to be perfect. You need to be present, visible, intentional, positioned.

You need a mindset shift and a practical roadmap.

So let's talk about the five precision moves that make up The Career Ninja Mindset™: **Plan, Prioritize, Practice, Persistence, Passion.**

It starts with **Planning**.

I'm not talking about the rigid, every-detail-in-a-spreadsheet kind of plan. I'm talking about clarity, a clear direction, a decision to stop winging it and start moving with purpose.

When I was promoted and moved from New York to Chicago, I knew that showing up and working hard wouldn't be enough. I had to build relationships, get buy-in, establish trust.

So I made a plan: team events, casual conversations, strategic collaborations. I even pretended to like Chicago deep-dish pizza. (Let's be real, it's not pizza, it's a casserole, but I sacrificed for the mission.)

That's the power of a plan. You stop hoping things will work out and start making them happen.

Next up is **Prioritizing**.

Many of us are drowning in to-do lists. We're juggling a thousand things, but never actually moving the needle. It feels like we're sprinting on a treadmill, exhausted, and going nowhere fast.

That's why you must ruthlessly prioritize.

Focus on the work that drives outcomes. Handle quick tasks immediately. Tackle the hard stuff first. ("Eat the frog," as they say. Again, no animals will be harmed, I promise.)

Don't start your day cleaning your inbox for the sixth time or rearranging your desktop folders. Start with the thing you're avoiding, the one that has the most impact.

Momentum comes from intentional movement in the right direction.

Then there's **Practice**.

Practice isn't glamorous, but it's absolutely crucial. You need to stay up to date and set realistic milestones for your growth. This takes time, and one of the mistakes we can make is to get too comfortable and stop sharpening our skills. Celebrate small wins along the way. Small victories add up and keep you motivated for the long haul of career advancement.

You've got to stay at the top of your game, and that's the difference. The people who succeed aren't the ones who know everything on day one. They're the ones who stay curious.

In today's world, 35 percent of the skills you use today will be outdated in five years. The only way to stay ahead is to stay hungry.

Now let's talk about **Persistence**.

We all want the straight line to success, the beautiful story arc, but in truth, sometimes life throws you a plot twist you didn't see coming.

You finally feel like things are falling into place, and then—boom: layoffs, market crash, investment gone sideways, dream job falls through. Something significant like that can throw you off the rails.

I've been there.

And what I've learned is that persistence isn't about grinding through everything blindly. It's about being in love with the process. It's about staying in the game even when it gets hard, even when it gets quiet, even when it gets slow, because often, the breakthrough comes one step past the breakdown. You pick yourself up off the floor and find the breakthrough. It's right there.

Last but never least: **Passion.**

So many people stay in jobs they hate because they're scared of the unknown. They say things like, "At least it's stable," or "Maybe next year things will change."

Meanwhile, the world is shifting under their feet. Companies restructure. Leaders change. Entire industries evolve, and you realize you've traded excitement for "safety" in a situation that was never safe to begin with.

When you follow your passion, you create energy, and that energy creates opportunity.

I've seen it in my own journey. From corporate banking to real estate to coaching, every leap I took started with asking, "What do I actually *want?*"

During the pandemic, my cousin and I went from casually chatting about a vacation to launching a real estate business in thirty days. It didn't happen because I had a perfect plan. It happened because I followed the fire.

And speaking of fire …

When I was a kid, I was responsible for keeping our house warm with a coal stove. This is not a metaphor, it was a real stove and real fire. If it went out, I would get in trouble, because that was one of my after-school chores.

So I had to tend it. Feed it. Pay attention to it, because if that fire died, I would lose my phone privileges, which at the time was the end of the world.

And here's what I know now: Your career is the same as that coal stove. You've got to feed the fire.

If you stop paying attention, if you let it burn out, you'll find yourself cold, stuck, and wondering why you are so unhappy.

But the good news is you can always relight it.

So I'll leave you with one final question.

Are you promotable?

Not "Are you qualified?" Not "Are you nice to have around?"

I mean, are you positioning yourself to be the person people can't help but think about when an opportunity opens up?

Because that's what being invincible really means.

And if you're not showing up like that yet, don't worry. You can start today.

The five precision moves to win at work—Plan, Prioritize, Practice, Persistence, Passion—aren't just concepts. They're your Ninja tools. They're how you stop playing small and start taking up space, because the truth is, you're already remarkable. You're already worthy.

Now it's just time to act like it. Put these concepts into practice and see what can happen for you.

You, my friend, are more than ready to become invincible.

ALEXIS KING

Alexis King, MBA, is a Certified Professional in Talent Development CPTD® career coach, speaker and passionate advocate for helping people achieve success. With over two decades of experience in L&D and the tech industry, Alexis has managed large international teams, delivered corporate training, and supported professional growth across industries. She is the creator of a 5-step process called The Career Ninja Mindset®, a strategic framework that empowers people to achieve their goals. Her own career path is a powerful example of this- moving from banking to tech, from employee to entrepreneur, and into real estate investing. With contagious optimism, Alexis believes that success isn't about chasing the next title- it's about being seen, valued, and capable of thriving in any environment.

www.AlexisKingConsulting.com

YOUR PSYCHIC AWAKENING: THE PATH TO TRUE TRANSFORMATION

Miwa Mack, Founder of the Boulder Psychic Institute

I want to tell you a secret.

Not a cute inspirational meme kind of secret. I'm talking about *the* secret—the one that, once you understand it, changes everything.

It's this:

As ***above***, *so below.*

That's it. That's the code. The blueprint. The ancient truth behind how your life unfolds.

When you change your spiritual energy—your "above"—your physical reality—the "below"—shifts to match it. Not through force. Not through hustle. But through resonance. This is when life starts feeling less like you're dragging yourself uphill and more like you're swimming downstream. You're still moving, still evolving—but with momentum, with grace. With ease.

Most people? They're trying to do the opposite. They rearrange their to-do lists, switch careers, remodel their kitchens, redo their morning routine… hoping their insides will eventually catch up.

But that's a backward equation:

*As **below**, so above.*

Real transformation doesn't start by moving furniture or buying new planners. It starts by shifting your energy at its source.

And here's the wild thing: You already have access to that source.

You don't need to earn it. Or prove yourself worthy of it. You don't need more crystals or perfectly written affirmations. You **are** spirit. You've always been spirit—even while living in a human body.

So now you find yourself overwhelmed. Sensitive. Hopeful, but hesitant. You know there's more to life than laundry, email, and existential spirals. But no matter how many podcasts you binge or vision boards you glitter, something deeper still feels… misaligned.

And if you're being really honest?

You don't want to struggle anymore. You want to know which path leads to ease. To face change with confidence, not dread. Maybe— just maybe—you want to stop fearing death so you can finally, fully live.

You're not broken. You're not imagining things. You're not "too sensitive." You're just spiritually untrained.

It's like someone handed you a beautiful instrument—your intuition, your knowing, your energetic awareness—and then never taught you how to play. So you walk through life hearing the melody faintly in your chest, but never quite able to bring it into song.

That's why I founded the Boulder Psychic Institute.

To teach people how to play the instrument their soul already knows. To turn whispers into trusted guidance. To help you manage your energy, develop your gifts, and finally, *finally* stop wondering if you're just making it all up.

Because you're not.

You're tuning in.

And this isn't just about seeing auras or decoding vibes—though, yes, you'll get really good at that, too. It's about becoming someone who can feel truth and walk through chaos without absorbing it. Who can stand in the middle of the noise and still hear the melody of their own soul.

But let me be clear—this didn't all start with a business plan or a flash of lightning on a mountaintop. It started with clouds.

Literal clouds—around people's bodies. I later found out that these clouds were auras.

I grew up in Japan, where being psychic wasn't considered strange. As a child, I saw auras. I felt everyone's emotions. I talked to ghosts. (Let's just say slumber parties got interesting.) I didn't know this was NOT normal—my grandmother supported me, asked questions, and even introduced me to real psychics.

But like so many of us, I shut it down. By the time I was eight, I could still see the clouds around people's bodies but everything else faded. I was trying to fit in. To survive.

Until I turned nineteen and everything came back. *All at once.* It was like my third eye had gone from dial-up to high-speed, and I couldn't unplug. I stopped driving. I stopped leaving the house. I thought I was losing it.

So I did the only thing I could think of… I opened the phone book looking for psychiatric help. And then it happened. This woman's name grew out of the page—like one of those nineties 3-D posters—remember those? The name just rising up to me.

And I thought, "Well, I think this is the person I am supposed to call."

At the time, I thought she was a *psychiatrist*. She turned out to be a *psychic*. And she asked me a simple question that changed everything:

"Would you like help managing your spiritual abilities?"

That was the beginning. She didn't give me answers. She gave me *practice.*

While she mentored me in how to give psychic readings and healings while also teaching me how to be sane as a person who "sees dead people," I was getting my degree in electrical and computer engineering (so, yes—I understand circuitry, both spiritual and literal).

But I soon realized that working as an engineer in cubicle-land was going to kill my soul. So I decided to hang out with the most psychic people on the planet—toddlers. My dream was to support young children in fostering their innate psychic abilities. I wanted to prevent them from losing these abilities like I did, but it turned out the biggest obstacle was the parents' fear of the unknown aspect of this work.

That's when I realized I needed to pivot and open a school—a community—where parents and really, all people, could learn what their souls already know but forgot. A place where sensitivity isn't a liability, but a superpower.

So in 2003, I opened the Boulder Psychic Institute.

Today, my vision is bigger than a school. It's a full-spectrum spiritual ecosystem—from conscious conception to peaceful death—where people are supported in staying connected to their gifts every step of the way.

Because I believe we're all born psychic. It's not a special gift. It's a birthright. And when we learn how to use it—everything changes.

Now, I want to offer you a deeper understanding of the principles that guide this work. Because when we understand how energy really works, we stop fighting life... and start dancing with it.

Let's begin with something simple—but powerful:

What you envision creates your reality.

That's not a cute idea—it's a law. Just like gravity. Just like electricity. What you envision for yourself becomes the energetic blueprint for what you experience.

This is nothing new. Athletes do this all the time. They visualize that hole in one or the three-pointer. And then they nail it! They don't just *hope, think,* or *feel* the win—they *see* the win and **manifest** it. Boom!

But the question isn't: *Can* you manifest?
The question is: Are you doing it with *purpose?*

Because if your energy is wrapped around fear, lack, or worst-case scenarios, you're still manifesting—you're just building castles out of chaos. But when you are focused on possibility, presence, and joy? Life starts to meet you there.

This isn't about pretending hard things don't exist. It's about choosing your creative direction.

Every single day.

Now, let's clear something else up.

There is no "good" or "bad" energy.

There's just... energy.

I used to think differently. I watched *Star Wars*, believed in light versus dark, good versus evil. But when I really started paying attention, I noticed something: Energy isn't moral. It doesn't come with a label.

Even in physics, a "negative" current isn't evil—it just flows in the opposite direction of a "positive" one.

So instead of judging energy (labeling it as good or bad), try asking: Is it in the right place? Take mayonnaise for example—it isn't good or bad (I love it with fries) BUT in your car's gas tank? Disaster.

Same with energy. Your energy belongs in *your* body. When someone else's energy is taking up space inside you, or yours is leaking into their field, things go haywire.

And the truth is, most people are walking around energetically scrambled. Picking up other people's feelings, thoughts, fears. Carrying burdens that were never theirs to begin with. No wonder you're exhausted.

But you don't need to analyze it to death. You don't need to spend three years in therapy unpacking your boss's passive-aggressive email.

You can just say: *That's not mine. Out you go!*

Because the goal here isn't to dig through your mental or emotional dumpster. It's to reclaim your own frequency—your *sovereignty*. And when you do, the shift is real. Tangible. Sometimes even instant.

Now, let's talk about your body.

You are not broken. You are designed for success.

Your body is not a malfunctioning machine. Your body isn't an illusion or something to overcome. Your body is your greatest spiritual teacher; it is how you get to experience everything here on earth and acquire wisdom.

So stop beating up on yourself. Those love handles are just fine!

All those negative thoughts? They're not part of your design. *You* would never pick on yourself. Those are other people's energies infiltrating your head—and they don't belong there. No judgment. But like the mayonnaise, they're just in the wrong place.

All those uncomfortable emotions. Same thing: incorrect placement.

You have been conditioned to believe that your body is the problem. But the truth is, your body wants to support you, like the most loyal dog in the world. Your job is to take the reins and become buddies with your body by managing its energy, so you can have all the success in your life.

You can even give your body "treats" when it does a good job (like sex and chocolate)!

Now, let's chat about the number one tool for managing your energy.

Grounding.

Grounding isn't spiritual fluff. It's spiritual *self-defense*.

We ground our homes, our power grids, even airplanes—to neutralize power surges and unwanted energy. Your body is no different.

When you're ungrounded, you absorb chaos. You feel fried. You lose your center.

But when you're grounded? You're resilient. You feel things without drowning in them. You witness pain without absorbing it.

You become *unshakable*.

You come home to your body.

It's what allows your intuition to become action. What transforms knowing into doing.

You see, the magic is in descending—not ascending.

Which leads me to one of my favorite reframes:

Your body is not a meat suit. (Seriously, can we stop calling it that?)

Your body is the *mold* for your spirit. The sacred container your soul chose to pour itself into. And most of us are not in our bodies, spilling our power all over the place—into old arguments, future fears, and unresolved childhood dynamics.

But your body? It's always in the now. And the now is the only place you can heal. And the present is the only place you can manifest.

So allow yourself to descend into your body. Let all of you arrive here, in this moment, in this form. Because when you are fully here—soul and body aligned—you become potent. Clear. Whole.

That is the true spiritual task: not to escape the body, but to *embody* the spirit.

To practice oneness within.

To choose presence.

And finally… let's talk about the thing no one wants to say out loud:

Energetic constipation is real.

Yep. I said it.

We're emotionally backed up. Spiritually bloated. Carrying energy we've stuffed down for years. We've been conditioned to treat our bodies like trash cans. Any time we don't know what to do with a feeling, a thought, or someone else's emotional outburst—we just stuff it down.

And then it shows up as fatigue, anxiety, or a total lack of motivation.

But underneath it? You're carrying what was never meant to stay.

And here's the truth: **You don't need to process what's not yours. You just need to release it.** You don't have to dig through your emotional dumpster. You don't have to decode every dark thought that pops up, just let go of what doesn't belong.

And when you do? Your system starts to flow again. You get clarity. You get focus. You get your *self* back.

Because your body is not designed to be a landfill.

It's designed to be a vessel for your light. Your life.

Now, if you are still with me—I want to leave you with a reality check.

Being psychic doesn't make you superhuman. I still get into weird arguments with my husband. I still have days where I feel like a soggy rice cracker—neither crunchy nor cute.

This work? It's not about being invincible. It's about being human.

This isn't about retreating from the world. It's about becoming so rooted in your spiritual truth… that the world starts to feel like home.

Not about constant joy—but steady peace.

Not about being above the human experience—but fully, beautifully *in* it.

Because when you remember who you are—and you learn to hold your energetic sovereignty, your truth, your presence—you become someone who doesn't just witness miracles...

You **manifest** them.

So if your spirit is nodding along—even just a little—I invite you to take the next step.

Come find your people.

Come remember your gifts.

Come let your soul pour fully into your life.

Come experience the magic of —

As above, so below...

MIWA MACK

Miwa Mack founded the Boulder Psychic Institute in 2003 to help spiritually curious people awaken their intuition, access their healing gifts, and consciously live from their spiritual power—within a safe, welcoming, and wildly supportive community.

A former engineer and lifelong student of how energy shapes every experience, Miwa brings a rare blend of precision and play to the spiritual arts. Her unique methodology and course design are rooted in decades of direct psychic observation, gained through volunteering in hospice care, prisons, psychiatric facilities, and supporting families as a preschool teacher and birth doula.

Miwa's pragmatic and systematic approach has helped thousands of students transform sensitivity into strength, emotional chaos into clarity, and indecision into confident action.

www.BoulderPsychicInstitute.org

THE 3C FRAMEWORK: STORY-DRIVEN CONTENT THAT CAPTIVATES AND CONVERTS

Barbara Mannino

Miss Class Sunshine. That was how they described me those many years ago when I graduated from Westfield High.

Yes, really.

In the yearbook—on the Senior Superlatives page—there I am, standing under an umbrella with Jimmy Smith, my male counterpart. We're both wearing raincoats and galoshes, flashing giant, beaming smiles like we just invented sunshine. Mister and Miss Class Sunshine.

That yearbook photo didn't just capture a teenage grin—it captured a truth that has followed me my whole life. Your smile, your energy, the way you show up in the world—it draws people to you. It's magnetic. And for me, that magnetism wasn't just the sunshine smile. It was the stories.

Even before high school, people would say, "That Barbara—she can tell a story."

And I could. Still can.

Telling stories isn't just something I do. It's who I am. It's the thread that has sewn together every season of my life, and the very foundation of my business today. My ability to tell a story has changed my life, enriched it, and helped me turn dreams into realities. And here's the best part: It's not just my superpower—it can be yours, too.

Because the right stories attract the right clients.

Let that settle for a moment.

And here's a secret that makes it even more delicious—when you find and tell those stories, you start to delight in them. They become less like marketing and more like magic. They stir up joy, laughter, gratitude. They make your heart sing. And as you delight in your stories, something beautiful happens—you empower yourself. And as you grow in that empowerment, you find more stories. And the cycle continues.

I call it the Circle of Story, a circle of delight, of authenticity, of momentum. It's alive and growing and full of possibilities.

That's what I want for you.
Not just to tell stories—but to be a story.
To wear your story like my mother wore her purple coat—with pride, with joy, with utter fabulousness.

Because when you do, everything shifts. Your confidence rises. Your message clicks. Your clients connect. Your business grows. And yes, your income grows, too.

Let's be honest—if you're reading this, there's a good chance you're not attracting the clients you want. Maybe your offers are being met with crickets. Your social media feels more like an echo chamber than a community. You're not closing the calls. You're not getting the leads. You're not being seen.

And that's painful. I've been there.

But here's what I know: Story can change that. Story will change that. Stories draw people in. Stories make them stay. Stories close the gap between you and your audience faster than any sales script or social funnel ever could.

Now, maybe you've heard this before. Maybe you've even tried to "tell your story" the way they say you should. But it felt awkward, like trying to do the splits when you haven't stretched in twenty years.

Point is, even if you think you can't tell a story, you can. But I want to offer you something more powerful than just a technique. There are people out there who will help you tell a story. Me? I help you *be* the story.

Because when you become the story—when your message, your presence, and your brand align into one unforgettable essence—you no longer chase clients. You magnetize them.

This didn't just come to me out of nowhere. I've lived it.

I was the kid with the notebook and the crayons. I became the editor of the Rough Rider in middle school. In college, I wrote for the PR office. And then—somehow—I ended up in banking. Probably for the money. It didn't last.

Eventually, I landed at a weekly newspaper, climbed the ladder, wrote for the global financial press, and even for Fox Business. I interviewed incredible people, told their stories, and gave voice to what mattered.

Later, I entered corporate America, doing everything from newsletters and branding campaigns to executive speeches. But corporate life eventually began to pinch. It was time to tell a new story. Mine.

So, I stepped out on my own. And as I found my voice, I discovered something amazing: When I told my story, people listened. Clients showed up. My business grew.

Today, I get to help others find their story and live it out loud. People say things like, "Barbara, you captured my voice perfectly," or "You added the dynamite." One even said, "You made me feel ten feet tall."

People tell me that, too, which is hilarious, because I'm five-foot-two on a good day.

But the truth is—I've never felt taller than when I'm fully in my story.

With a clear voice and aligned message, you don't just get seen—you get chosen. And that leads to profit.

Because when you work with me, we don't just craft content—we transform it from flat messaging into full-bodied story experiences that connect deeply and inspire action.

That's what I want for you.
Because when you wear your story like a custom-made coat—stitched with your values, your voice, and your vision—you don't just show up ... you shine.

Let's talk about that coat.

Your brand is your story coat. It's the single most important investment you can make in your business. Not the funnel. Not the Facebook ads. Not the new website colors or fonts. Your brand.

Because your brand is what people say about you when you leave the room.

Picture it: You're at a dinner party, and you step away to take a call. The minute you're gone, people start talking. What they say—that, my friend, is your brand.

So let's rewind.

Before anyone can talk about your brand, you need to make sure they understand it. Your brand should tell a story. A real one. One that evokes emotion and builds connection. When you communicate your brand with purpose and heart, people remember you. They feel something. That's the secret sauce.

And here's where it gets fun—storifying your brand.

Let's say you're a local bakery. You don't just sell pastries. You create joy in flaky, buttery layers. You bring back someone's childhood memory with a bite of almond croissant. You create warmth and community in a paper box tied with string.

That's story. That's brand. That's what people buy.
Because people don't just buy products. They buy stories. They buy you.

Now, let's go deeper. Content is your storefront. It's how you show the world who you are, what you believe, and why you matter. Without content, your business is invisible—like a store with no sign, no lights, and no door.

But with great content… you've got neon lights, a welcoming glow, and the scent of something irresistible wafting out into the street.

I call it the Content Experience—content that doesn't just inform but transforms. It makes your right client think, "Wow, this person gets me."

Your content should reflect your brand's story, but in bite-sized, soul-filled pieces. Maybe it's a social media post that makes someone laugh and cry at the same time. Maybe it's an email that feels like a handwritten letter. Maybe it's a video where you share a tiny personal moment—and someone else feels seen for the first time.

That's not marketing. That's magic.

Let's make it practical. When your content speaks to "what's in it for them"—WIIFT, as I love to call it—your audience listens. Not because you're being clever, but because you're being clear. They can see the value. Feel the connection. Smell the croissant.

And clarity, my dear, is queen.

Which brings me to my three essential storytelling pillars: Curiosity, Clarity, and Captivation—my 3C Framework.

Curiosity is the spark. It's what drives you to ask better questions, to explore your journey, to listen for the heartbeat behind your own story. It helps you find the gold hidden in the everyday.

Clarity is the structure. It's what turns a meandering monologue into a purposeful message. Without clarity, your story is just noise. With clarity, it becomes music.

And Captivation? That's the magic dust. It's the part that draws people in, that makes your voice linger in their minds long after the scroll has stopped. It's the emotion, the rhythm, the sparkle.

When you tell your story with Curiosity, Clarity, and Captivation, you don't just communicate—you connect. You create community. You convert.

But here's the part no one tells you: You have to be comfortable in your own skin to do this well.

And for many of us, that's the real work.

The fear of being judged. The fear of failure. The fear of not being good enough. It's like background music in the heads of too many brilliant people. And that fear? It dulls your shine. Muffles your voice. Shrinks your presence.

You don't have to let it.

When you become comfortable in your own skin, your fabulous just is. You don't have to chase it. You don't have to manufacture it. It flows through you.

That's what made my mother unforgettable.

Her name was Peg. And in the last year of her life, she wore this glorious purple coat. I can see it now—her white hair, her perfect little wedge heels (yes, even while cleaning the house), and that radiant coat.

She loved it. She said it made her feel fabulous.

And people remembered it. Years later, they still talk about "that purple coat."

That coat wasn't just fashion. It was her story.

It made her feel bold, bright, full of life. And when she felt that way, she shared it with everyone around her. Her story lit up the room before she even said a word.

That's the legacy I want to help you create.

I want to take the fabric of your life—your ideas, your values, your experiences—and sew them into something wearable. Something powerful. Your very own story coat.

A story that fits you perfectly. A story that draws people in. A story that makes you proud to show up exactly as you are.

You already have everything you need. The moments. The meaning. The magic.

You just need someone to help you stitch it together, slip it on, and strut a little.

Because when you wear your story well, you don't just show up for your business—you show up for your life.

And oh, how fabulous that is.

So here's what I want to leave you with:

Stories are everything.

They're everything for *your business*, yes. They help you get clients, grow revenue, and make a difference.

But stories are also everything for *your life*. They help you savor the small moments. They help you fall in love with your own path. They help you connect, transform, and remember who you are.

They help others see you.

And more importantly, they help *you* see yourself.

So go out there and be the story.

Live it. Share it. Wear it.

It will change your business—and it just might change your life.

BARBARA MANNINO

Barbara Mannino is the founder of The Content Experience, creator of the 3C Framework, and a content experience expert. Using Curiosity, Clarity, and Captivation, she helps leaders and businesses turn their story into content that connects, converts, and drives real profit. A former journalist for Fox Business and global financial media, and a senior communications lead for Fortune 500 firms, Barbara transforms flat messaging into full-bodied experiences that elevate presence, amplify voice, and spark action. She speaks on branding, storytelling, and authentic presence. Barbara helps clients stop chasing visibility and start creating content that moves people—and markets.

www.BarbaraMannino.com

"Mari's story made me cry, laugh, and then sell my first $6K coaching package—with just one sentence she helped me write."

— *Sarah L., Energy Healer Coach*

SCRUBS OFF, SALES ON: FROM NURSE TEARS TO SIX-FIGURE CHEERS WITH WORDS SHARPER THAN A SCALPEL

Mari McCann, Nurse-Turned-Message Surgeon™

The operating room lights buzzed overhead, blinding white. Cold dry air pumped from the ceiling vents, like the hospital was trying to refrigerate its staff along with the patient on the table. I could smell iodine. Burned skin. Latex. Blood. I was standing on the same tile square since sunrise, holding the rib spreader. Arms locked. Elbows screaming. Back aching. Feet numb in plastic clogs designed by a sadist with a grudge against toes. Not charting. Not prepping meds. I was the human clamp. Again.

Third surgery that day. Eight hours deep. No break. No water. Just a three week-old peppermint in my pocket I decided to keep. I had named it. My emotional support mint.

The surgeon cracked a joke about tequila and interns. Then, without turning, said, "Is she still standing back there?"

Still standing? Oh, I was still standing. Still saving lives. Still choking on exhaustion. Still getting paid like I worked at a gas station sandwich shop, next to the scratch-off tickets and microwave burritos.

But here's what no one tells you in nursing school: You can be the calm in the chaos … and still be the one bleeding out.

I was the implementer. The invisible force. The good girl in scrubs who followed orders, anticipated needs, made sure nobody flatlined. Except me.

Because quiet excellence? Doesn't save you. And sacrifice? Only benefits those who never pay you back.

And yet… I stayed. Because I believed the lie: Work harder, they'll see you. Give more, they'll reward you. Show up earlier, stay late, they'll finally say, "You matter."

But two decades in, all I had to show for it was foot pain, frozen ambition, and a pension that wouldn't buy a decent bottle of wine or cover the therapy I needed after HR was done with me.

Worst part? I still thought I owed them more. Maybe you've felt that, too, giving everything to a system that only returns silence.

The hospital doors hissed shut behind me. Cold. Final. Like the system spitting me out. I stood frozen. One hand on my car door. The other clenched around my hospital badge like it still meant something. I didn't move. I just stood there. Like the world had ended, and no one noticed.

Rage was doing gymnastics in my chest. My breath shallow. My ID tag dangling uselessly like a dog collar.

Twenty years. Ten-hour shifts. Birthdays missed. Weekends traded for overtime.
Silence became the default for survival.

And for what? A whisper campaign. A manager too spineless to stand up. A betrayal so quiet it almost felt polite.

That day, I didn't just lose a job. I buried her: the good girl in scrubs. The one who thought sacrifice earned safety. The one who believed hard work meant protection.

Maybe you've known her. Maybe you are her. Maybe your breakdown didn't happen outside a hospital. But maybe it was a bathroom floor. A walk-in closet. A locked car.

You know the place. The tears. Not the soft kind. The steering-wheel-bashing, mascara-melting, rage-weeping kind. And then … silence.

That was the moment. When grief met clarity. When the voice I buried under policies and people-pleasing finally screamed: "No more!"

And right after I screamed it, guess what showed up? Fear.

Not the monster-under-the-bed kind. The mortgage kind. The "what if I'm not enough?:" kind. The part of me that whispered, "You're not the speaker. You're the nurse."

But another voice started rising, quiet at first, but clear: "Not anymore."

I didn't know what came next. I just knew I wasn't going back.

Because no one teaches you this in the operating room.
If you want to save a life…
You might have to start with your own.

That was the moment I buried the good girl in scrubs.

Six months later, I showed up at a business event in worn flats and a fresh chip on my shoulder. The ballroom smelled like printer ink, perfume, and hotel coffee. Lanyards everywhere. People buzzing, swapping cards, snapping selfies, talking leads. I stood in the back with a thick notebook, feeling like a new nurse with the wrong binder. I almost left the room.

I came for strategy. I didn't know I was about to meet ... me.

Then she walked out. Suzanne. Oversized glasses. Bold. Unapologetically her.
She didn't hold a mic. She was the mic. The way she commanded the room, you'd swear she had two - one for strategy, the other for soul.

And she didn't coddle. She sold fire. Her words hit like a defibrillator with no warning. Not motivational. Surgical.

"Clarity is currency," she said. "Confusion doesn't convert. You want to get paid? Find your voice."

She wasn't speaking to me. She was calling me out.

If you've ever heard someone say exactly what your soul needed to hear, like they reached in and named the ache, you know what I mean.

At that moment, I didn't just hear a business strategy. I heard my *epiphany*.

I realized I'd spent two decades driving the wrong vehicle. My old one? Nursing. Saving lives with scalpels. My new one? Messaging. Saving entrepreneurs with their own story.

I didn't need another degree. I didn't need a new plan.

I needed a mic. I needed a message. I needed to stop being the scalpel ... and become the surgeon of my own story.

Maybe you don't need another credential either. Maybe what you need is permission to stop disappearing.

I didn't want to be the backstage implementer anymore. I wanted to be seen. Heard. Paid. Not for my labor. For my language.

I wanted to help others say the thing they couldn't find the words for. Because once I saw what the right words could do?

I chose something.
Visibility.

The stage I was never invited to. The truth I never gave myself permission to tell. Because my story was valuable.

The hospital pushed me out. I pushed publish - and made my first $6K with words sharper than a scalpel.

Here's what they, and I, didn't expect...

The woman who was pushed out the side door of the hospital walked straight into her own spotlight, carrying a message sharp enough to make her first $6K in a day. I made more in less than three weeks than I used to earn in three months elbow-deep in someone's intestines...

No retractors. No orthopedic shoes. No *Yes, doctor*. Just me. My story. And a message that finally paid what my degree never could.

Let me show you what changed everything: a ladder. The same one I used to climb out of burnout and into a business built on my voice.

The Scalpel to Spotlight Ladder™
Every client I help falls somewhere on this ladder.
Maybe you do, too.

Level One: The Operator
You're the hands. The doer. The implementer. You hold it all together ... and no one sees you. Ten hours deep, rib spreader in

hand. Everyone hears the monitor beeping, but not your heart. You're praised for endurance. But invisible in the rooms that count.

I was so good, I became invisible. My name was in no report. But my body? It bore the bruises.

You know what exhaustion tastes like. It tastes like resentment marinated in silence.

Level Two: The Coordinator

You manage the doers. You've earned the clipboard, the title, maybe a parking spot. You keep the chaos running smoothly, but it still owns you.

Anna, one of my clients, was here. Leading a team. Booked solid. Secretly Googling "Is burnout real?" We cleaned up her message. Nailed her 10-minute talk. She closed a $10K client in one conversation. Structure's nice. Clarity pays better.

Because burnout doesn't need more meetings. It needs a message with muscle.

Level Three: The Mover

You pick up the mic. Not because you're polished, but because you're ready to be real. Your story becomes your strategy. You're not waiting. You're building your own podium.

Jess came to me with two programs, a dozen ideas, and zero clarity. We sliced the extra. Shaped one offer. One talk. Within one week, she had one offer, one clear message, and a new $5K client. No website. No sales page. Just her truth, well-spoken.

She didn't need a funnel. She needed words that worked.

Burnout doesn't need more hustle. It needs clarity that finally pays.

Level Four: The Maker

You don't just speak. You create. Frameworks. Movements. Messages that live on. You're not just in the room. You own it. When you speak, people lean in, because your words don't just inspire … they sell.

Barbara? Sold out her group offer in two days. Yvonne? Found clarity in minutes, not months.

Since then, I've helped coaches close $5K, $10K, even $36K offers, without a fancy funnel. Just clarity. Just the right words. Because when your message is sharp, it sells before you finish the sentence.

The next time someone asks what you do, will your words sound like a whisper, or a wire transfer?

You don't need more followers or funnels. You need a message that pays your mortgage and moves your mission.

So where are you? Still clamping open the chest for someone else's vision? Or ready to grab the scalpel and carve your own?

This ladder isn't just mine. It's ours. And the moment you stop climbing someone else's version of success? You start rising on your own.

I'm not here to help you speak louder. I'm here to help you speak with precision.

Your story? It's not cute words. It's a revenue-producing, spotlight-seizing, soul-rescuing instrument. And if you've been waiting for permission to pick it up? This is it.

Cut deep. Cut clean. Cut through.

Don't just turn the page. Turn your voice into value.

Because the next name in this book might be good—but the world's waiting for yours.

Because the person reading this right now? He/She's not just one good message away from more confidence, he/she's one sentence away from being seen.

Mari McCann
Nurse-Turned-Message Surgeon™
I don't hand you frameworks. I hand you the words that pay. You bring the fire.
I bring the scalpel. **Together, we cut straight to the sale.**

MARI MCCANN

Mari McCann is the *Nurse-Turned-Message Surgeon*™. For 25 years, Mari held scalpels and silence. She stood in the Operating Room, steady hands, unseen heart, keeping lives open while her own voice stayed closed.

Today, she helps fast-action coaches and entrepreneurs trade burnout for truth, turning buried stories into powerfully paid messaging. Known for words sharper than a scalpel, Mari doesn't just help you find your voice, she hands you the mic.

If you've ever felt like the backstage operator in someone else's success story… Mari is the woman who helps you cut through fear, claim the spotlight, and speak your value into income.

www.MariSMccann.com

THE REAL WEIGHT YOU'RE CARRYING ISN'T ON THE SCALE

Debra Overdorf

Turns out—you can't hate yourself into health.

If shame burned calories, we'd all be supermodels. But that's not how this works. Not for you, not for me, not for anyone. We've been fed a lie for decades: If you want to lose weight, just "eat less and move more." That's it. End of story.

Except it's not.

What they never tell you is the part that actually matters—the part that explains why none of the spreadsheets, apps, or color-coded containers ever seem to *stick*.

They forget the third step: feel worthy.

And honestly? That's where most of us are stuck.

Not in the pantry.
Not in the snack aisle.
But in the soul-sucking glow of the dressing room mirror, trying on jeans clearly designed by someone who hates women *and* denim.

You know the ones. The tag says size 8, but your self-esteem says, "No, ma'am."

Or maybe you're like I was—deep in the grind, hyper-committed to every rule and every regimen. You've done it all: keto, paleo, SlimFast, Whole30, cabbage soup, celery juice, that one Jennifer Aniston swears by. You've calculated macros like you're solving for x in a calculus equation just to figure out what you can eat for lunch.

And still... something feels broken.

You've eaten protein like its penance. Chewed each bite with the focus of someone mad at their life and their chicken breast. But the number on the scale doesn't reflect the effort, the sacrifice, the obsession.

So you keep searching.

You think, *Maybe I haven't found the right thing yet. Maybe there's a secret I missed. A better order for the supplements. A better app. A better plan.*

But deep down, if you're being honest, you don't really think the problem is the plan.

You think the problem is *you*.

You think you've failed. That you've overlooked something. That you missed your shot. That you're the broken one.

You tell yourself, *If I could just lose the weight ... then everything would fall into place. The job. The relationship. The peace of walking into Target and trying on jeans without having a full-blown spiritual crisis in the fitting room.*

It all hinges on the number.

The one on the tag. The one on the scale. The one in your head that tells you what you're worth.

But here's the truth bomb no one ever handed you: You are not broken.

You are not some walking project in need of constant fixing. You don't need to be punished into progress. You need to be loved into healing.

Because no amount of kale—no matter how organic, free-range, or sung-to-by-moonlight—will heal a body being fueled by self-hate.

And once you stop trying to earn your worth and start remembering that you *already* have it? That's when the transformation begins. I know this, because it happened to me.

I'm not here to sell you a new "magic combo" or talk about carbs like they're criminals. I'm here to help you come home to yourself. To your body. To the part of you that's always been worthy—even if you forgot for a while.

Because the real weight? It's not what's on your plate.

It's the decades of stories you've been told—stories that say you're not enough. That you must shrink to be loved. That you must hustle to be worthy.

It's time to drop those stories. And replace them with the only truth that matters: You were never broken. You just need to remember who you are. And love yourself back to life.

So how do we make this shift—from punishment to partnership, from restriction to radiance?

It starts with one thing: We stop dieting.

No more weighing your lettuce. No more treating your kitchen like a chemistry lab. No more eating steamed broccoli while whispering affirmations and trying not to cry.

You stop punishing yourself. You start *listening*.

Listening to your body. Listening to your hunger. Listening to the quiet voice inside that asks, *"What if I'm already enough?"*

That's where we begin. Because true transformation happens from the inside out.

If your job title disappeared tomorrow, would you still know who you are? Or would you be like I was, standing in the kitchen, holding a spoon, trying to remember what you came in there for?

We're so busy performing our roles—mother, partner, employee, boss, crisis negotiator, emotional support human—that we forget who we were before the roles were assigned.

And here's the kicker: You can't show up for your life if you don't know who you are in it.

So we take inventory. What lights you up? What makes you roll your eyes so hard they could detach? What do you want—not what your kids want, or your partner wants, or your boss expects—*but you*?

You have to peel back the layers. And when you do? You find out you're not just worthy.

You're kind of spectacular.

Then we break the cycle of dieting.

I once tried a juice cleanse so extreme I nearly proposed to a bag of pretzels. That's not health. That's a hostage situation.

You weren't born to count almonds or cry into a rice cake. You were born to *thrive*.

So we ditch the crash diets and build real nourishment—anti-inflammatory meal plans designed for your hormones. Food that fuels your energy, not drains it. A rhythm of eating that supports your life, instead of shrinking it.

And because food isn't the whole story, we also talk about movement.

Not punishment. Not "run until you can't feel your emotions" workouts. But joyful, intentional movement.

Dancing in your kitchen counts. Especially if there's hip action.

We build a movement plan that works for your body, your schedule, and your energy. We include strength, mobility, sensuality. We create morning rituals that ground you before the day steamrolls you.

And we add in somatic release—because your body holds memories. Stress. Shame. Every awkward email you've ever reread ten times.

You get to let that go.

But here's what really changes the game: boundaries.

If you're constantly saying yes while your soul is screaming, *please say no*, we've got to fix that.

I give you scripts. Actual words. For how to say no to your boss, your sister, your inbox.

We even do a "Bold No" challenge, so you can practice guilt-free boundary-setting with a little sass and a lot of support.

Because here's the deal—your time and energy are not renewable. You don't get a rebate for burnout. You don't get a trophy for exhaustion.

You are allowed to protect your peace.

And once you're clear on who you are, what you need, and how to fuel your body with love?

We move into visibility.

Yes, *that* kind. The kind where you walk into a room and don't instantly regret your outfit, your posture, or your decision to exist in public.

We create embodied confidence. We start with style—not the trendy, exhausting kind, but the *strategic* kind. The kind that makes people lean in and say, "There's something about her."

We identify your style archetype. We build looks that reflect your truth. You don't need more clothes. You need clothes that feel like *you*.

Then we layer in visibility rituals. Tools to help you show up on Zoom, on stage, in meetings, in life—with presence, not panic.

Because how you show up … shifts everything.

And once the inner and outer transformations begin, we don't just high-five and move on.

We *anchor it*.

This is about sustainability. About integrating new habits into your real, messy, beautiful life.

We celebrate the wins—big and small. We keep you grounded. And we create a lifestyle that honors everything you've become.

Not a phase. Not a fad. Not a temporary fix.

But a foundation.

You have the tools. You've done the work. And now? You get to *live* like the woman you've become.

And I'll be real with you—I didn't learn all this in a textbook.

I started my career as an executive assistant. For thirty years, I gave everything to my job. I was on international calls at 2 a.m., coordinating flights from Qatar, scheduling the unschedulable.

I was the go-to, the get-it-done girl. I had a spreadsheet for everything—except my own life.

My health fell apart. My adrenals tanked. I didn't gain weight so much as I accumulated it like frequent flyer miles.

And I kept thinking, *If I could just lose 15 pounds ... maybe I'd finally feel safe. Maybe I'd be loved. Maybe I'd be enough.*

Even when I became a pastor—yes, I was a pastor's wife for twenty-one years, and a pastor myself—I was still running on empty. Preaching fire on Sundays and burning out by Monday.

It wasn't until I hit rock bottom that I realized I was my own ideal client.

I enrolled at the Institute for Integrative Nutrition—not to become a coach, but to save myself.

And now? I teach what I lived. I lead women home to themselves.

Not with gimmicks. Not with guilt.

But with joy.

Because when you stop counting calories and start counting love and joy, you don't just lose weight, you gain your life back.

I want to leave you with this: Follow your healing.

Follow that whisper inside—the one that says,
"I want to feel good in my body."
"I want to wake up with energy."
"I want to look in the mirror and see joy instead of judgment."

Because I believe this with everything in me:
When women take back their health, they take back their lives.

You stop living at the mercy of the scale.
You stop outsourcing your worth to a number.
You stop apologizing for your size, your presence, your brilliance, your voice.

You *rise.*

Not because you hit some arbitrary goal weight.
But because you remembered who you were underneath all the noise.

This isn't about shrinking.
It's about *becoming.*

Becoming more you. More joyful. More vibrant. More alive.

So if you only do one thing from this moment forward—please, do this: Take care of your body.

Not because you're trying to earn your worth. But because you finally know you already have it.

Take care of your body like it's your most beloved home. Like it's the only one you've got. Like it's listening—because it is.

Because every time you nourish yourself, move with intention, set a boundary, speak your truth, or simply rest—you are saying, *"I love you"* to yourself in the most powerful way possible.

And when you lead with love?

Everything else follows.

And if something in you whispers, *"This is it..."*

Then I want you to listen.

Count what really matters.

Because when you stop counting calories—and start counting love and joy—you don't just lose the weight.

You gain *you*.

DEBRA OVERDORF

Debra Overdorf is a Certified International Health Coach who specializes in helping ambitious women level up in both their professional and personal lives—specifically at the powerful intersection where executive success meets lasting wellness. With a passion for guiding high-performing women to achieve vibrant health without sacrificing their careers, Debra is on a mission to show that it's possible to thrive in both corporate and daily life.

She is the International Best-Selling Author of Beyond the Scale: Emotional Healing from Food Addiction. Her coaching style is direct, compassionate, and deeply empowering. Whether she's working one-on-one, leading group programs, or speaking on stage, Debra inspires women to take bold action in their wellness journey—no matter how busy or overwhelmed they may feel. Her message is clear: your health is not a side hustle to your success—it's the foundation of it.

When she's not coaching or speaking, Debra is a passionate advocate for women's health, a lover of nutritious food, and a believer in the power of emotional healing to unlock lasting change.

www.HealthCoachDebra.com

BODY DEBT™: THE INVISIBLE COST OF SITTING STILL AND HOW TO RECLAIM YOUR ENERGY, INFLUENCE, AND INCOME

Laura Ribbins

Sitting is the new smoking.

That's not a catchy headline or a dramatic overstatement. It's real, backed by data, and deadly serious.

Researchers have shown that sitting for more than eight hours a day—without physical activity—puts you at the same mortality risk as smoking. Let that sink in. Your chair might be more dangerous than a pack of cigarettes.

And guess what? We are sitting. A lot.

Nearly half of employed adults describe their workdays as mostly sitting. Thirty-six percent don't engage in *any* leisure-time activity. Zero movement. Zero motion. Zero momentum. Less than 5 percent of us hit just thirty minutes a day of movement. And the effects? Devastating.

We're talking about 22 percent of coronary issues. Twenty-two percent of colon cancer. Eighteen percent of osteoporotic fractures. A spike in diabetes. Hypertension. Breast cancer. The numbers are grim.

But you don't need a spreadsheet to tell you something's off.

You feel it.

You're stiff. Your back aches. You're skipping meals because you're "too busy." You're parked at your desk, hunched over your keyboard, caffeine in hand, living in a blur of Zoom calls and to-do lists. And somewhere along the way, your health has quietly slipped into the back seat.

You're drained. Frustrated. Sluggish.

And maybe—if you're really honest—you're wondering if this is just how it has to be when you're running a business or trying to stay afloat in your career.

I'm here to tell you, it doesn't.

In fact, I believe something radical: **When business owners lose weight, they find money.**

Yes, really.

Because you can't build an empire if your body's falling apart. You can't grow your revenue if your energy's tanked. You can't lead a team, serve your clients, or chase your vision if you're constantly running on fumes.

I've seen it again and again. The moment someone commits to their health—when they move their body, feed it well, change the way they think—their business shifts. Their relationships shift. Their finances shift. It's not magic. It's not a miracle. It's the natural result of finally showing up for yourself.

And before you think, *Well, that's easy for her to say* ... let me give you a peek into why you might want to listen to me.

I've been in the health and wellness space for over forty years. I'm not new here. I've taught, trained, choreographed, competed, and coached around the globe. I'm a two-time bestselling author. A four-time Ironman competitor. An international fitness presenter and master trainer. I've taught thousands, trained thousands, moved with thousands.

I've also raised two Olympians. Built a swim program. Been awarded Fitness Professional of the Year by the American Aquatic Association. And I've walked the walk every step of the way.

But beyond all of that, I'm also the daughter of a ninety-six-year-old woman who still hikes with me in Yosemite. Who raised me with a rule: If the sun's out, you don't sit inside. She's the reason I move. The reason I teach. The reason I believe in what I do.

And listen, if you're doing the math, you'll realize I've circled the sun quite a few times myself. But I feel like I'm forty. I live like I'm forty. Because I've built my life around what I teach.

Here's what I know: There is a better way.

A way where you don't trade your health for your hustle. A way where you don't sacrifice your energy to chase your income. A way where the body you live in *fuels* your dreams—instead of fighting them.

And it doesn't have to be hard.

We're going to talk about three simple pillars: **mindset, movement, and nutrition.** Foundational shifts that can unlock everything you're working toward.

But first, I want you to understand this: I don't just have credentials. I have compassion. I've worked with people who thought they were too far gone. Too old. Too tired. Too overwhelmed. And I've watched them come back to life.

So if you're feeling stuck, frustrated, or like you've lost yourself somewhere between deadlines and dinners … I see you.

Let's find a new path. One where you lose the weight, gain the energy, and yes—find the money.

Let's begin.

*   *   *

Let's start with the piece no one wants to talk about, but everyone needs: **mindset.**

Your mindset sets the tone for everything else—how you eat, how you move, how you show up for your business, your body, your life. If that internal voice is filled with "I can't," "I'm too old," or "It's too late," then it doesn't matter what diet or workout you try—it won't stick.

The truth is mindset isn't something you find. It's something you *choose.*

Sometimes that choice comes from a shift—a moment of clarity, a quote, a video, a conversation that sparks something inside you. Maybe it's watching Dr. Joe Dispenza on YouTube. Maybe it's a story that reminds you of your own strength. The source doesn't matter. What matters is that you stay open. Curious. Willing.

The right mindset isn't about perfection. It's about believing you can take the next small step. And that's where transformation begins.

Then there's **movement.**

This isn't about pushing your body to the brink. It's about reconnecting to it.

Maybe that looks like walking outside. Gardening. Yoga. Cleaning your space with music blasting. Whatever gets you breathing, stretching, sweating—even just a little.

The key is to fall in love with the feeling movement gives you. That rush of energy, that buzz of aliveness. And there's a bonus: When you do it in community—even virtually—you multiply the benefits. We need that now more than ever.

Next, we've got **nutrition.**

This isn't about restriction. It's about fueling your body with real food that supports real energy and healing.

Whole foods. Fresh ingredients. Simple choices that add up. Not to be perfect—but to feel better. More alive. More alert. More *you.*

Nutrition isn't just about what you cut out. It's about what you *bring in.*

Then there's something I see too many people ignore: **self-education.**

Staying mentally sharp isn't optional—it's vital. Read. Listen. Learn. Challenge your brain like you challenge your body. You don't have to go back to school, just stay curious. The world is your classroom.

Finally, let's talk about **community.**

We weren't meant to do this alone. Whether it's a class, a retreat, a coaching group, or a daily text from a friend—we need connection.

Your health journey doesn't have to be lonely. In fact, it's more powerful when it's shared.

And just like teaching a baby to swim, building a healthy life takes guidance, patience, tools, and support. You don't have to jump in and flail. You get to learn—with someone who knows how to get you there.

Someone like me.

*   *   *

I started this chapter with some pretty rough statistics. The kind that make your stomach drop. The kind that leave you thinking, *"What am I even supposed to do with all that?"*

So let's flip the script.

Let's talk about what's *possible.*

Losing just 5 to 10 percent of your body weight? That small shift can significantly reduce your risk of heart disease, type 2 diabetes, and even certain cancers. Just a few percentage points in the right direction—and your entire future changes.

Getting just one hundred fifty minutes of moderate movement per week—that's a thirty-minute walk five days a week—can lower your risk of diabetes by 58 percent. That's more than most medications can offer.

Reducing belly fat? That can mean deeper, better sleep. Fewer interruptions. Less snoring. Less sleep apnea. More waking up feeling rested, instead of worn out.

And then there's the emotional side. Weight loss isn't just about the scale. It's about your mental health. Your self-esteem. Your confidence. People report reduced depression symptoms, a more positive self-image, and a renewed sense of ownership over their lives.

There's even research showing that maintaining a healthy weight can help you live longer.

Just ask my mom.

Ninety-six years old and still saying yes to hiking, boat rides, and new adventures. Still moving. Still engaged. Still *thriving.*

That's not a fluke. That's the power of consistency. Of movement. Of choosing nourishment. Of prioritizing connection. Of keeping your mind sharp and your spirit engaged.

That's the power I want for you.

You don't have to overhaul your life overnight. You just have to take the first step. Choose to shift your mindset. Choose to move a little more today than you did yesterday. Choose to put something nourishing on your plate. Choose to stay curious. Choose to reach out and connect with people who will walk this path with you.

Because you were not meant to wither away behind a desk.

You were not meant to run on caffeine and willpower and call it success.

You were meant to feel good in your body. To feel strong, capable, and confident. You were meant to build a business *and* build your health. You were meant to wake up excited about what's ahead—not dreading what your body won't let you do.

So let's stop sitting still.

Let's stop waiting until "later."

Let's stop pretending that our bodies don't matter.

They do.

You do.

I've helped babies learn to swim, and I've helped adults reclaim their energy, their health, and their joy. Whether you're stepping into the shallow end or ready to dive deep, I'm here to help you learn to swim in the waters of wellness.

And yes, along the way … you just might find a whole bunch of money at the bottom of the pool.

Let's get moving.

Let's get thriving.

Let's go.

LAURA RIBBINS

Laura Ribbins is a globally recognized fitness and wellness expert based in Grand Cayman with over 40 years of experience. A four-time Ironman athlete, award-winning presenter, and founder of the Aqua-Kidz swim program, she's led thousands toward better health through movement. As a Master Trainer and holistic lifestyle coach, Laura helps business leaders and entrepreneurs reverse Body Debt™—the hidden toll of a sedentary life—and reclaim energy, confidence, and independence. Through her signature blend of movement, mindset, and nutrition, Laura empowers people to move well, live well, and age with strength and freedom.

www.SuccessWithLaura.com

THE MISSING VITAL SIGN: WHY COMPASSIONATE CONVERSATIONS ARE THE KEY TO THRIVING TEAMS AND HEALTHIER SYSTEMS

Karen Rigamonti, MD

What *is* this?

How much money do you make?

When are you going to settle down?

When are you having a baby?

Who are you voting for?

Do you know what they do to this?

Are you really wearing that?

We all know these questions—the ones that make the air thick at family dinners, where the mashed potatoes grow cold and the room shifts from warm to unbearable. They're the kinds of questions you learn not to ask, but they still show up, uninvited and disruptive.

And yet, even in conversations where we're not being interrogated, we often find that something's missing. Connection. Understanding. Kindness. Vulnerability. Real listening.

I saw this in my own home.

We were having dinner just the other night. My husband was discussing some global issue. My oldest daughter—the lawyer—was dissecting the legal implications. My younger daughter—the physician—added an archaeological angle. And my son—the one with disabilities—chimed in with his own jibber jabber. Each person brought their brilliant passionate voice to the table.

And I sat there ... feeling completely lost.

Not because I couldn't follow their logic, but because no one was *listening* to one another. Everyone was speaking. No one was being heard. And that realization hit me like a wave.

This—this dinner table chaos—is exactly what the healthcare system feels like.

Fragmented. Frustrated. Full of voices yet starving for understanding. Brilliant dedicated people operating in silos. Conversations layered with urgency but stripped of compassion. Systems that talk at each other, not with each other.

In today's healthcare environment, you don't have to dig deep to find the pain.

Doctors. Nurses. Receptionists. Administrators. Technicians. Schedulers. Executives. They're all carrying more than meets the eye.

Stress. Burnout. Isolation. Disillusionment.

Understaffed and overtasked. Underappreciated and overwhelmed. Morale evaporates, retention plummets, errors rise, satisfaction falls.

And yet—everyone is trying.

Everyone wants to deliver excellent care. Everyone wants patients to feel supported. Everyone wants their colleagues to feel safe, heard, and respected. But good intentions are forgotten under pressure. People are asked to do more with less. The joy they once felt in their work gives way to dread. And in the middle of it all, patients and families—real human beings—slip through the cracks.

It doesn't have to be this way.

I believe with every fiber of my being, healing happens when we start with *compassionate communication*. When we remember that the people in our systems—patients, yes, but also staff—are not just job titles or data points or walking diagnoses.

They are human.

And when we speak to one another from that place—when we really listen, when we create space for vulnerability, when we stop defaulting to blame and start choosing empathy—everything begins to shift.

I've lived this truth.

As a mother of three, one of whom lives with profound disabilities—including autism, blindness, and intellectual delays—I've spent more than three decades advocating for children and families within healthcare, education, and community. I've seen what happens when people are dismissed. I've seen what happens when they are included.

Besides being a physician and family caregiver, I've also been a grandmother. A coach. A researcher. A partner in global healthcare initiatives. I've worked alongside executives, caregivers, physicians, and staff in high-stakes environments like ORs, ICUs, and emergency rooms. And I've witnessed the cost—financial, emotional, and spiritual—of broken communication.

But I've also seen what's possible when people decide to change the culture.

During my time at a healthcare joint venture in Saudi Arabia, we set out to do exactly that. Shift the organizational culture. Make it more person-centered. Make it more disability-centered. At first, it wasn't easy. I was blocked from coaching and consulting. I had to advocate not only for others—but also for myself.

But I knew it was worth it.

Because when we trained not just the doctors and nurses, but the ancillary staff—housekeeping, nutrition, laundry, groundkeeping— we saw something extraordinary. People who had never been included were suddenly brought into the conversation. I led a workshop with nearly a thousand of them. Their response moved me to tears.

They felt seen. Heard. Valued. Many told me it was the first time anyone had asked them how they felt.

That moment affirmed something I've always known:

Everyone has the capacity to grow, contribute, and care—if we create the conditions that allow them to.

When the hell of the healthcare system has an advocate for compassionate communication, healing happens.

And I am that advocate.

*　　*　　*

Let's talk about communication—but not the surface-level kind.

I mean the kind built on compassion, transparency, and deep listening. Because in healthcare, most breakdowns don't happen from a lack of intelligence or intention. They happen when people stop hearing each other.

It's easy to fall into silos. Easy to move fast, assume, react. But those moments of disconnection carry a cost: missed opportunities, mistakes, burnout, and pain.

What if we could shift that?

What if we chose to speak with courage and listen with presence? What if we stopped just reacting and started responding—with empathy?

It starts with presence. Then honesty. Then accountability.

Are we showing up as who we really are—or hiding behind our titles and roles? Are we naming what's real—even when it's hard? Are we taking responsibility for how we impact those around us?

These small shifts, when practiced consistently, change the way teams function. They change how patients feel. They change outcomes.

But communication isn't just about words. It's also about emotional intelligence—something I return to again and again in my work.

Self-awareness. Self-acceptance. Self-care.

These aren't buzzwords. They're the foundation of resilience.

Self-awareness asks us to look in the mirror and see clearly—not just our strengths, but our patterns. Self-acceptance allows us to meet that reflection with compassion. And self-care? It's the ongoing commitment to treat ourselves with the same respect we offer others.

Without these, we run dry. We lose the ability to lead, to collaborate, to care.

This is especially true for leaders. Because leadership isn't just about direction—it's about presence.

I once walked the wards with a chief nursing officer who wasn't getting honest feedback from her staff. With a few adjustments to her approach, everything changed. She didn't just hear "fine" anymore. She heard the truth. And more importantly, she responded to it—right there, in the moment.

That's what real leadership looks like. Not perfection. Presence.

And part of leading well is building a culture that embraces learning—even when mistakes happen.

That's the essence of "Just Culture."

In a Just Culture, we stop asking, "Who messed up?" and start asking, "What went wrong in the system?" We separate human error from reckless behavior. We treat people fairly. We learn together.

Fear stifles innovation. But fairness unlocks it.

When people feel safe to speak, to question, to own their learning— we create something powerful. A culture that evolves. A workplace that heals. A team that thrives.

And beneath it all is connection.

Not just connecting to policies or processes, but to people.

Because when people feel seen, they show up differently. They contribute more. They trust more. And the entire system benefits.

I saw this in a thousand-person workshop I led for ancillary staff— people often overlooked. But when they were invited to the table, they lit up. They contributed. They grew.

And I've seen it in my own life. In my son—who is blind, autistic, and limited in intellect—standing onstage and singing a few precious words with confidence. I'll never forget that standing ovation.

It reminded me that everyone, no matter their circumstance, deserves the chance to be heard. To shine. To feel included.

And that starts with compassionate communication.

Before we wrap, I want to leave you with a quote I hold close.

Epictetus, the Greek philosopher, once said, "We have two ears and one mouth so that we can listen twice as much as we speak."

It's simple, isn't it? But deeply true.

In the busy corridors of our hospitals, in conference rooms filled with tension, in the private quiet of patient care—there is one thing that has the power to transform everything: listening.

And I don't mean the kind of listening that waits for its turn to speak. I mean the kind that leans in. The kind that seeks understanding. The kind that hears the fear behind the frustration, the pain behind the silence, the longing behind the pushback.

That kind of listening is sacred.

It's also the foundation of compassionate communication—and the first step toward healing not just patients, but systems, staff, teams, families, and whole communities.

When we truly listen, people feel seen. When we speak from compassion instead of compliance, we build trust. When we show up vulnerably and consistently, we shift culture from the inside out.

The work isn't always easy. Sometimes it's exhausting. Sometimes you'll wonder if anyone else is even trying.

But I promise you this—when you make space for connection, when you speak truth wrapped in empathy, when you build bridges instead of walls … something begins to heal.

You begin to heal.

Your team begins to heal.

Your organization begins to heal.

And yes—your patients begin to heal, too.

This is what I believe with every cell in my body: When the hell of the healthcare system has an advocate for compassionate communication, healing happens.

That's the work I do.

And if you're reading this and thinking, *I want that for my team,* or *I want to be that kind of leader,* or even just *I want to feel human again inside the system I work in*—you're not alone.

Let's sit around the proverbial dinner table and talk.

Let's talk about how to bring humanity back into healthcare.

Let's talk about how to create environments where everyone— patients, staff, families—feel safe, respected, and supported.

Let's talk about how to lead with integrity, communicate with compassion, and build systems that don't just run, but thrive.

If you're ready to begin, I'm here.

Because healing doesn't happen in silence.

It begins with a conversation.

Let's have it.

KAREN RIGAMONTI

Dr. Karen is a physician, coach, and culture reformer transforming healthcare from the inside out. With an MD, MPH, MBA in Leadership, and advanced coaching credentials, she works with providers and organizations to create systems that treat people—not just diseases. A caregiver and mother to a son with disabilities caused by medical error, her personal mission fuels her professional impact. Her proven methodology bridges gaps across patients, professionals, and administrators—boosting retention, engagement, and outcomes. Internationally recognized, Dr. Karen brings compassion, clarity, and change to every level of healthcare. Learn more at https://drkaren.org.

www.DrKaren.org

THE "READY" DELUSION AND WHY YOUR BOOK CAN'T WAIT

Karen Strauss

Have you ever read a book that cracked something open in you?

Maybe it was a story that gripped your heart, a business book that lit your mind on fire, or a memoir that made you feel less alone. Maybe it was a dog-eared paperback you picked up at the airport, or a hardcover you proudly gifted a friend. Maybe you've caught yourself peeking at someone's bookshelf just to see who they really are.

Books are woven into the fabric of our lives. They sit on nightstands and coffee tables. They fill bags and hearts. They teach, entertain, awaken, and heal.

I love books. Always have. I love the way they smell, the way they feel in my hands, the way they ask nothing of me but my attention—and then reward it tenfold.

But let me ask you something a little more sensitive: Do you want to write a book?

Not someday. Not maybe. Do you want to write a book now?

Because if you do, you're not alone. Around 80 percent of Americans say they want to write a book. Most never start. Only a small fraction—about 3 percent—actually write one. And less than 1 percent get it published.

The odds are daunting, yes. But here's the thing: The people who *do* write and publish books? They change their careers. Their visibility skyrockets. Their confidence deepens. They get more clients, more speaking gigs, more credibility—and yes, more income.

Writing a book positions you like nothing else can. It's one of the most powerful credibility tools an entrepreneur, coach, or thought leader can have.

And it's not just theory for me.

I've spent nearly four decades in publishing—at houses like Random House, Macmillan, and Crown. I've worked every angle—sales, marketing, publicity—and in 2011, I founded Hybrid Global Publishing to help entrepreneurs, experts, and creatives bring their books to life.

I've seen firsthand what happens when a book lands. When the message clicks. When a reader finishes the last page and thinks, *I need to work with this person. I trust them. I believe in them.*

I've helped authors hit bestseller lists. One of my clients sold thirty thousand books in a single day and debuted at #4 on *The New York Times* list. When he came to me, he was already a known journalist—but his book had stalled. I told him what others wouldn't: You've got to let people see you. The vulnerable you. The human you. He did. And the public ate it up.

That's what a book can do, but only if you get it out of your head and onto the page.

And that's where most people get stuck. Not because they don't have something worth saying—but because they don't know how to say it, how to shape it, or how to get it published.

Let's change that.

I want to introduce you to someone: Lynn Young.

Lynn came to one of my Big Leap retreats with a strong desire to write a book—and absolutely no idea how to start. Her mind was overflowing with ideas, stories, themes. All good stuff. But there was no center. No clarity. No through line to tie it all together.

She was, in her own words, a creative mess.

But I could see it—buried under the noise was a voice, a message, and a book people would love. So we got to work. We talked. We listened. We shaped the big idea. Then we outlined the structure. And then, Lynn wrote.

She wrote through grief. Through challenges. Through life. She kept showing up. And that persistence paid off.

Her book, *Red Hot Living: Becoming a Joyful Badass Sager*, became a #1 Amazon bestseller. Readers called it "a joy," "pure feminine energy," "a page-turning journey to the authentic self."

And just like that, people started coming to me asking for "The Lynn Young Treatment."

But what they were really asking for was this: Help me make sense of my message. Help me claim my purpose. Help me write the damn thing.

Because once you know what your book is *really* about—and why it matters—everything else gets easier. You stop second-guessing. You stop procrastinating. You stop letting fear drive the bus.

But there's another place people get stuck, and it's this: They don't know *how* they'll publish the book. And that uncertainty paralyzes them.

Publishing is a world full of options, and not all of them are equal. So let me break it down for you.

There are three main publishing paths: traditional, self, and hybrid.

Traditional publishing is what most people picture. Big publishers, literary agents, editorial teams. You submit your manuscript or proposal, cross your fingers, and hope someone says yes. If they do, they'll handle the editing, design, and distribution. It's prestigious—but it's also hard to break into.

Self-publishing is the opposite. You do it all yourself. You write it, you hire your own editor and designer (please, *hire* an editor and designer), and you publish it via Amazon or another platform. You keep control, but you're also the full marketing and logistics team.

Then there's hybrid publishing—my lane. It's a blend. You retain control and ownership, but you get real publishing support. Professionals help you with editing, design, marketing, and strategy. You pay for services, yes—but you avoid the amateur-hour pitfalls of low-quality self-publishing and the gatekeeping of traditional publishing.

Now here's the twist: The publishing path you choose will shape *how* you write your book.

Traditional? You'll need a proposal and maybe just a few chapters to start. Self-publishing? You'll need a finished manuscript and a solid production plan. Hybrid? We walk with you the whole way.

So before you write the whole book, take a minute to choose your path. That one decision can give you clarity, confidence, and momentum. And I want you to have all three.

When a new client comes to me unsure where to start, I guide them through a simple but powerful filter I call **The Five Whys**. It helps uncover the real reason they want to write a book—and that clarity changes everything.

So let's walk through them.

First: Is this a passion project? Maybe you have something in your heart that just won't leave you alone. A topic or idea that you feel *called* to explore, no matter how many copies it sells.

Second: Do you want to build your authority? A book can make you the go-to voice in your field. It says, "I know what I'm doing," before you even walk into the room.

Third: Do you need to share your story? You've lived through something powerful, and you know others could benefit from hearing it. This isn't about ego—it's about impact.

Fourth: Are you looking to grow your business or increase your income? Books can absolutely support that. They can act as high-converting lead magnets, brand builders, even back-end sales tools.

Fifth: Do you want to expand your network? Books open doors—to new partnerships, new clients, new circles of influence.

Once you know your why, you'll write with purpose. You'll make smarter decisions about structure, voice, marketing, and publishing. You won't get as easily derailed by fear or perfectionism.

Speaking of fear, let's call it out.

The number one thing that keeps would-be authors stuck isn't time. It's not money. It's not skill.

It's the belief that they're not enough.

Not smart enough. Not experienced enough. Not young enough. Not old enough. Not *anything* enough.

"I don't know how to write a book."

"I'm not a writer."

"No one cares what I have to say."

That voice in your head? It's lying to you. And I say that with love.

You *do* have something to say. And people *do* care—if you're willing to meet them halfway and share with heart, clarity, and honesty.

And here's a little secret: You don't need to write a perfect first draft. You just need to write *a* first draft.

Anne Lamott calls it the "shitty first draft," and she's right. You get to write badly at first. Sloppily. Disjointedly. Your only job is to get the words down. You can't edit a blank page, but you can absolutely refine a messy one.

Give yourself permission to start imperfectly. That's how every great book begins.

Now that you're ready to write, there's one more roadblock we need to clear: deciding *what* to write.

It sounds obvious, but trust me—it's where so many people stall out.

They don't know if they should write a memoir, a business book, a how-to guide, a self-help book, or something in between. They feel pressure to say everything, which means they say nothing clearly.

Here's my take: Don't try to blend everything into one book. It rarely works.

If you're a business owner with a compelling personal story, use your story to support your business message. Don't make the story the whole point. Readers want to see *themselves* in what you write. So tell stories—but only the ones that connect to the bigger message your reader cares about.

And once you've made your decision?

Start writing.

Don't wait for the perfect first line. Don't wait for the ideal writing environment. Don't wait until you've "figured it all out."

Just start.

Because here's the real heartbreak: Too many people sit down to write and then ... freeze. They look at the blank screen, and it stares back. They get up to get a snack. They check their email. They reorganize their desk. They tell themselves they need to "get in the zone."

And the book doesn't get written.

That can't be your ending.

You've got a message worth sharing. You've got a story worth telling. You've got wisdom someone else is waiting to receive. And you don't have to do it alone.

Let me help you.

Let me help you start writing. Let me help you stay motivated. Let me help you structure your message, get it on the page, and move it into the world with confidence.

Let me help you publish it the right way. Market it effectively. Sell it smartly.

Let me help you turn your unwritten idea into a finished book.

Not next year. Not someday.

Now.

Because the book you're dreaming about?

It's ready for you to start writing it.

And I'm ready to help you do it.

KAREN STRAUSS

Karen has held various positions in the Publishing industry for over 35 years. She worked at Random House, Macmillan, Crown, and Avon in Sales, Marketing, and Publicity. She has worked with celebrities such as President Jimmy Carter, Jimmy Stewart, Martha Stewart, George F. Will, and Og Mandino.

In 2010, Karen founded Hybrid Global Publishing, a firm that works with Entrepreneurs, Speakers, and coaches to help them write, publish, distribute, and promote their books in order to generate unlimited leads, get on more speaking stages, and grow their business by attracting more clients.

Karen has helped over 1000 business owners become successful published authors and has helped 700 authors reach #1 bestselling status.

www.HybridGlobalPublishing.com

WHAT IF THE LAST CHAPTER IS THE BEGINNING?

Tina Y. Weller

I stumbled across a list the other day—"The Top 40 Most Annoying Things a Spouse Does". You'd think I'd roll my eyes and scroll past it, but I didn't. I clicked. I read. And I laughed.

Snoring. Leaving clothes on the floor. Burping like a teenager at a sleepover. Watching videos at full volume. Oh, and, of course—leaving the toilet seat up. Classic.

Somewhere between "hair in the sink" and "wet towels on the floor," I smiled and thought, *Yup, been there.*

And don't even get me started on the things children do. It was funny ... until it wasn't.

Because here's the thing: Once they're gone—really gone—you'd give anything to step on those socks again. You'd welcome the snore in the middle of the night like a lullaby. You'd practically celebrate finding a used towel abandoned on the bathroom floor. These little annoyances, the ones we used to huff about, become sacred memories wrapped in the scent of a person we loved.

When you lose someone—a partner, a child, a parent, a friend—your world doesn't just change. It fractures. There's the life before ... and

275

the life after. And in between, there's silence. Not just quiet. *Silence.* That kind that rings in your ears.

You make the tea, but there's no one to chat with while it brews. You drive to the grocery store, still reaching for their favorite snacks. You sit down at night and glance at the empty side of the couch, half expecting to hear their voice. Your routines stay the same. But you? You're different. You feel like half of something that used to be whole.

And here's the hardest part: You keep living by rules that no longer apply. You still don't spend money on yourself. You still don't go out. You still set two places at the table. It's like you're following a blueprint for a life that's already burned down.

I know this place. Not in theory, but in experience.

After my husband passed away from pancreatic cancer, everything in my life blurred. He had just retired. Sixty. Healthy, until he wasn't. One minute we were planning trips and projects. Next, I was planning his funeral. And even in the hollow aftermath, I still had children and my son. He became my anchor.

But then ... Four years later, I lost him, too.

My son had been living with Duchenne muscular dystrophy and was dependent on life-saving measures. Machines, nurses, constant care. I devoted my entire world to keeping him alive. That purpose consumed me in the most sacred way. And then suddenly, it was gone.

The house, once buzzing with beeping machines and busy nurses, turned still. I remember standing in the middle of it all, the silence pressing against me like a weight I couldn't lift. Thirty years of being his mom, his caregiver, his person—and now, I was just ... me.

And "me" felt like a stranger.

If you've ever experienced a loss like that—loss that rearranges your soul—you know what I mean. It's not just the grief. It's the question that follows you everywhere: *Now what?*

Because grief doesn't just take people. It takes identity. It takes purpose. It takes the future you were planning. And what it leaves behind is … fog. You don't know where to step, what to say, how to move forward. You're scared you'll forget them. But you're also scared of never feeling joy again.

I want you to hear me on this: You don't have to have it all figured out.

You just have to start where you are. In the mess. In the silence. In the space that feels too big and too empty.

There is a way forward. It won't be neat or easy or fast. But it's possible. And I'm here—not with a magic fix, but with a hand outstretched, ready to walk beside you.

Because while loss gives us no choice in what it takes, it *does* offer a choice in how we move forward.

And that's where our story continues.

Let's talk about that next.

Here's what I want to say first, and I say it with love:
You don't have a choice.

I know—that sounds harsh. Maybe even a little unfair. But stay with me.

When it comes to loss, we don't get a vote. It shows up uninvited, wrecking everything in its path. One day you're planning your week, the next you're planning for a world without someone you love. No warning. No preparation. No control.

You didn't choose this. You never would have.

But here's where the shift happens: You *do* get to choose what happens now.

Not in a "just be positive" kind of way. That's not what this is. This is about acknowledging that while you didn't ask for this story, you're still holding the pen. And you get to decide how the next chapter unfolds.

Choosing to move forward doesn't mean you forget. It doesn't mean you stop missing them. It just means you stop trying to rewrite the past. You put the question of *why* down—not because it stopped mattering, but because it's too heavy to carry every day.

And then, slowly … you take a step.

Maybe that step is making dinner for yourself. Maybe it's going for a walk. Maybe it's just getting out of bed. It doesn't have to be big. It just has to be *yours*.

And it's okay if grief comes with you. It doesn't have to stay neatly packed in the corner. Let it ride shotgun. Let it cry with you in the shower or sit beside you during dinner. Grief isn't the enemy. It's the evidence of your love.

And you can love someone and still choose to live.

That brings me to something else I've learned:
We all get the same twenty-four hours.

That truth hit me hard after my losses. Because there were days I couldn't get off the couch. Days when time crawled. And then other days, I'd blink, and the sun was setting. Time is strange when you're grieving.

But even in that strange stretch of time, one thing remained constant—those twenty-four hours were mine. I couldn't rewind them. I couldn't skip them. I could only decide how to live inside them.

And living didn't always look pretty. Some days it meant doing laundry. Some days it meant crying in the car. Some days, I just sat with a cup of tea and stared out the window. But I was still showing up.

You don't have to conquer the day. You just have to meet it. Grief can come along. So can joy. So can confusion. All of it is welcome. Because it's all real.

Another thing I want to tell you:

Everything you've done has led you here.

I used to look back and wonder if I missed a turn—if I could have done something, said something, chosen differently. That's a painful loop to live in. But over time, I started to see it differently.

Every moment, even the ones I didn't choose, shaped the woman I am now. And that includes the grief. That includes the heartbreak. It's all part of the story, even if I wish it wasn't.

You may not like this chapter. I didn't either. But it's still yours. And even here, even now, it's shaping you into someone more resilient, more compassionate, more awake to what matters.

That doesn't mean you need to be grateful for the pain. But you can be proud of what you've carried. You can acknowledge how far you've come—even if it doesn't feel like far enough.

And maybe, just maybe, you can start looking forward.

That brings me to one of my favorite reminders:
Your windshield is so much bigger than your rearview mirror.

It's no accident that the thing helping you see ahead is wide and clear, while the thing showing you what's behind is small and framed. The past matters, yes. But it's not the whole picture.

When we're grieving, the past takes up so much space. We replay moments, revisit words, reimagine endings. That's okay. That's human. But if you try to live by looking backward, you'll miss what's right in front of you.

Life is in the windshield. In the messy, unpredictable road ahead. That's where new joy lives. That's where healing happens. That's where you meet the version of yourself that's still becoming.

So glance at the past. Honor it. But keep your eyes forward.

And one last thing. I know how hard it is to ask for help—especially if you're the one who's always done the helping. When friends offer casseroles or company, you say, "I'm fine." But you're not fine. You're hurting.

What if, just once, you said yes?

Yes to dinner. Yes to the walk. Yes to someone folding your laundry. Yes to support. Yes to connection.

Right now, I'm offering you that yes.

This journey doesn't have to be lonely. I've walked it. I still walk it. And I want to walk beside you—not to fix anything, but to remind you that you're not alone. To remind you that it's okay to need support. That it's okay to live again.

Because here's what I believe with my whole heart:
They didn't choose to leave you.
And they don't want you to be stuck in sadness forever.

You honor them by living. By laughing again. By building something new, even while holding them close in your heart.

And you don't have to do it all today. You don't have to know how. You just have to say yes to the first step.

Say yes to healing.
Say yes to the possibility of joy.
Say yes to living what's next—even as you continue to accept what was.

We'll take it one step at a time.
Together.

TINA Y. WELLER

Tina Y. Weller is a Grief and Healing Coach who supports those navigating life after loss.

Drawing from her own experience of losing both her husband and son, Tina brings a rare blend of lived wisdom, psychological insight, and compassionate support. With a background in entrepreneurship, psychology, and energy healing, she helps others find clarity, purpose, and the courage to begin again. Through one-on-one and group support, Tina gently guides the grieving toward healing and the strength to live what's next—without letting go of what was.

www.JourneyWithGoodThings.com

THE PAIN REFRAME: HOW TO OUTSMART YOUR BODY'S OLD HABITS AND GET MOVING AGAIN

Jennifer Yagos

If toddlers could talk, we'd all be getting roasted.

"Why do grown-ups grunt when they stand up?"

"Why do they walk like malfunctioning robots?"

"And why—seriously—can't they sit on the floor without looking like they just lost a bet?"

And honestly? Those toddlers would be absolutely right.

Because let's face it—somewhere between snack time and tax time, many of us forgot how to move. We used to squat down to play, roll around for hours, leap off the playground like we had invincibility power-ups. Now we bend down and pull something. We sneeze wrong and need a chiropractor. We sit cross-legged and wonder if we'll ever walk again.

It didn't used to be this way.

Our bodies didn't betray us—we just stopped using them the way they were designed to move. We traded crawling for cubicles, play for posture, and recess for rush hour. But what if I told you that the flexibility, fluidity, and freedom you had as a kid isn't gone?

It's just sleeping.

And your brain? That brilliant little computer behind everything you do? It still remembers.

But here's what I want you to know: Your body isn't broken. It's brilliant. And your brain—your body's GPS—is just waiting for a new route.

Because the key to reducing pain and regaining mobility isn't just in your muscles or joints—it's in your nervous system. It's in how your brain tells your body to move, brace, compensate, and react.

Somewhere along the way, we unlearned how to move. We layered on tension, tightness, and fear. And that fear—of pain, of movement, of reinjury—rewired how we carry ourselves through the world. And that rewiring? It's often the root of our discomfort.

I see it every day. The client who can't sit comfortably anymore. The parent who wants to get on the floor with their kid but dreads the thought of getting back up. The high performer who powers through the workday, only to crash in a haze of pain and fatigue the moment they get home. I see the frustration in their eyes. The resignation. The quiet question behind the brave face: "Is this just how it's going to be now?"

No, it's not.

You're not stuck. You're not fragile. And you're certainly not a lost cause.

You're simply out of sync with the movement patterns your body once knew so well.

Think back to how children move. They don't wince when they twist or groan when they stand. They don't need a warm-up to run full speed toward joy. They're relaxed, curious, fluid. That's not magic. That's memory. That's efficiency.

And here's the beautiful truth: Your brain still has that memory. We just need to remind it.

You might be thinking, *Okay, great. So how do I do that? Do I need to find a jungle gym and some juice boxes?*

Thankfully, no. (Though I wouldn't stop you.)

What I teach isn't about reverting to childhood. It's about reawakening the innate intelligence of your body and nervous system—using small, strategic, mindful movements that speak directly to your brain's operating system.

The main way I do this is through the Feldenkrais Method®. Now, if you've never heard of that, don't worry. You're not alone. Some people think I've just sneezed when I say it out loud. But Feldenkrais® is a game-changer. It's about moving smarter, not harder. About teaching your brain to let go of pain patterns and return to ease.

No surgeries. No gritting your teeth through "no pain, no gain." No pushing until something pops.

Instead, we get curious.

We get quiet.

We listen.

And in that space—between old habits and new awareness—your body begins to shift.

*　　*　　*

Let's start with what I like to call the Whole Body Tune-Up.

You know how sometimes we treat our cars better than our bodies? We'll schedule oil changes, rotate tires, check warning lights. But when our neck starts hurting? We slap a heat pack on it and keep going. Lower back screaming? Maybe we stretch for thirty seconds while scrolling Instagram and call it "mobility work."

We've been taught to treat pain like an isolated event. Neck hurts? Fix the neck. Knee hurts? Blame your age and wrap it up. But here's the thing—your body isn't a collection of disconnected parts. It's one integrated, brilliantly adaptive system.

Ignoring that is like painting over a crack in the wall without checking the foundation.

That neck pain? It might actually be about your feet. Your stiff hips. Your posture. Or even the way you clench your jaw during stressful meetings.

Everything is connected.

And when one part goes offline, the rest of the system starts compensating. That's where the trouble starts. Compensations become habits. Habits become patterns. Patterns become pain.

So instead of chasing symptoms, we zoom out.

We look at the whole body. We ask better questions.

How do you stand? How do you walk? Where are you holding tension without even realizing it?

We don't attack the pain. We get curious about it.

This is where the Feldenkrais Method® comes in. Think of it as gentle movement meets neuroscience. You're not doing reps. You're not forcing a stretch. You're lying on the floor (or sitting or standing) and doing small, intentional movements that reawaken your brain's natural coordination.

Sometimes, it looks like nothing. But inside your nervous system? Fireworks.

You're sending new messages. Creating new connections. Telling your brain, "Hey, this movement is safe. This feels good. We don't have to guard anymore."

Because here's what most people don't realize: Chronic pain isn't just a body problem—it's a brain pattern.

And patterns can be rewired.

Which brings me to one of my favorite nerdy topics: neuroplasticity. (Don't worry, no flashcards required.)

Neuroplasticity is your brain's ability to change, adapt, and learn. Yes—even as an adult. Even if you've been stuck in pain for years. Even if you've been told "this is just how it is now."

Your brain is like a path in the woods. The more you walk a certain route—let's say, the one labeled "tight shoulders and stiff back"— the more defined it gets. But the cool part? You can carve out a new path. One built on ease. Fluidity. Awareness. You just have to walk it a few times.

And that's exactly what mindful movement does.

We teach your body new options. We build new roads. And suddenly, you're not just stretching—you're rewiring.

Because pain isn't just about movement. It's also about memory. Emotion. Stress. Your nervous system constantly scans for safety. When it senses danger—physical or emotional—it tightens up. Protects. Braces.

Which is helpful if you're running from a bear.

Less helpful if you're just trying to unload the dishwasher.

So we calm the system. We shift the signal. We train your brain to associate movement with comfort, not crisis. And when that happens, pain starts to fade—not because we forced it out, but because we stopped reinforcing it.

One of my favorite examples? I had a teenage client with scoliosis. He wasn't just in pain—he was also struggling to play his trumpet because of how his posture affected his breath.

We didn't "fix" his spine.

We gave him better options.

We explored how his body wanted to stand. How he could feel more grounded, more balanced. And guess what? His pain reduced. His sound improved. Because movement isn't just about mechanics. It's about freedom.

And here's where things get really fun.

Remember how I mentioned toddlers? How they move with ease, curiosity, and total trust in their bodies?

That's the goal.

Not to regress—but to return. To rediscover that natural, unfiltered way of moving through life. Because movement should feel good. It should feel playful. And it absolutely should not require gritting your teeth through a boot camp-style workout designed to "fix" you.

One of the most powerful tools I bring into this work is NLP— neurolinguistic programming. Think of it as the language of your subconscious. The internal dialogue that drives your actions, reactions, and physical responses.

Athletes use it all the time. They mentally rehearse their routines before they ever touch the equipment. And studies show that even imagining a movement can light up the same parts of the brain as actually doing it.

That's wild. But also wildly useful.

Because if we can shift the way you think about pain—if we can train your brain to expect ease, to visualize movement with joy instead of dread—we can change how your body responds in real time.

*   *   *

Here's something that might blow your mind: research shows that 60 to 80 percent of joint pain isn't caused by structural damage.

Let that land for a moment.

The stiffness. The aching. The sense that you're falling apart piece by piece every time you stand up too fast—it's probably not because you're broken.

It's because your movement patterns are.

And that? That's something we can change.

You don't need to be "fixed." You need to be reintroduced to your body's original settings. Not the ones layered in tension and compensation—but the ones built for ease, fluidity, and play.

But let me be clear—this isn't about pushing harder. It's not about becoming someone you're not. You don't need to lift heavier, run faster, or become some Insta-perfect yoga pretzel.

You just need to move like a kid again.

I don't mean swinging from monkey bars or doing cartwheels in the yard.

What I mean is moving without fear. Without flinching. Without bracing every time you bend, lift, or twist. Because somewhere along the way, most of us picked up habits that told our brain: "Movement equals pain. Movement is dangerous. Movement is the enemy."

We can flip that script.

And when you shift those patterns?

The impossible becomes possible.
The possible becomes easy.
And the easy … becomes elegant.

Let's get you back to moving with confidence. Not through force— but through awareness, curiosity, and small, smart changes.

You don't have to go back to being a toddler.

But your brain? It still remembers. Let's wake it up.

JENNIFER YAGOS

Jennifer Yagos helps people stop tiptoeing around pain and start moving with confidence again, no matter their age. With over 30 years of experience, she's the founder of Motion Freedom, where she blends the Feldenkrais Method® with gentle, brain-based techniques to retrain the nervous system and restore natural movement. Her approach is light on strain, big on results, and built on the idea that movement should feel good, not forced. Jennifer offers weekly online classes, private sessions, and digital programs to help people ditch the stiffness and rediscover ease in everyday motion.

www.MotionFreedom.com

STOP SINKING, START RISING: WHY YOUR SELF-WORTH, NOT YOUR SALARY, IS THE REAL GAME-CHANGER

Sue Yelvington

I once wrestled a 2,500-pound bull back over a fence.

Pregnant.

Holding a whip.

And all the men stood safely behind a fence and watched me do it.

Now, if that doesn't tell you something about who I am, let me say this: When people tell me they're wrestling with money issues, I nod—but quietly, I'm thinking, *Honey, I've wrestled with bigger.*

Because I have. I've wrestled with shame that stuck to me like wet clothes. With trauma that hid under my skin like a bruise I couldn't explain. I've wrangled the silence that comes when you don't know how to ask for help. The doubt that creeps in when you're almost out. The kind of advice that sounds loving but just tells you to shrink.

And here's what I've discovered after a lifetime of wrestling, rising, and rebuilding: Most people who feel stuck in their finances aren't struggling with money. They're drowning in meaning.

See, it's not about the numbers on a spreadsheet—it's about the story those numbers tell you about who you are and what you're worth.

My name is Sue. But around here, I'm known as "Unsinkable Sue." Not because life hasn't tried to take me under. Oh, it has—repeatedly and with enthusiasm. But because no matter how wild the waves get, I find my way back to the surface. I rise. And when I coach women around money, what I'm really doing is helping them rise, too.

Because when your self-worth is high, you become unsinkable.

And that's what this work is about. Not budgets. Not bank accounts. Not even your impulse buys on late-night Amazon scrolls. It's about your worth.

Most of us think we have a money problem.

We don't.

We have a self-worth crisis.

I've talked to women who say, "Sue, I've tried everything. I've downloaded every budgeting app. I've tried envelopes, side hustles, spreadsheets, essential oils I can't even stand the smell of. I've read the books. Listened to the podcasts. I even gave Bitcoin a shot, and now I just feel even more broke—financially and emotionally."

And when I hear that, I get it. Because I *was* that woman.

And I also know this: No amount of financial strategy can outpace the voice inside you that whispers, "You don't deserve this."

That inner voice? It will sabotage every budget you create, every financial goal you dare to set, and every win you try to celebrate.

So if nothing's working, it's not because you lack discipline.

It's because you've been trying to fix your bank account when what you really need to repair is your relationship with yourself.

And the wildest part? No one told you that.

You've been doing what they told you to do—get up earlier, hustle harder, save more, spend less. You've been following the strategy without understanding that strategy without self-worth is just another hamster wheel.

You don't need another financial planner. You need a mirror. One that shows you who you are underneath the money stress, the credit card guilt, the impulse purchases that feel like comfort but turn into shame.

You're not broken.

You're tangled.

In stories. In beliefs. In habits you never chose but absorbed anyway.

What we do together is gently trace that yarn back to its source. We find the moment—the memory, the message, the meaning—that's been running your life without your consent. And we untangle it. We tell the truth, the real truth. The one that sets you free.

Because I've seen this too many times to doubt it: The problem isn't your spending. The problem is that you're spending your peace trying to feel worthy.

Let me tell you a little about how I got here.

I didn't choose this work. It chose me. Or maybe it *grew me*.

I was seventeen the day I realized something had to change. I'd gained five pounds overnight—yes, *overnight*—and I stood in my kitchen in crisis. Not because of the weight, but because of the self-loathing it triggered.

That's when the lightning bolt hit: If I didn't learn to love myself fat, I'd never get slim.

That moment kicked off a lifelong journey of personal growth. And honey, once I started, I never stopped.

From there, life handed me plenty of material. I married a man with a heart condition, two kids, and a hostile ex-wife. I joined Mary Kay to stay home with the kids and earn enough to survive if he died. (Spoiler: He didn't die—we divorced.)

I moved into a rundown house with three kids, no plan, and more financial chaos than I care to admit. But I knew one thing: if I stayed in that marriage, my soul would die. So I left—before the money made sense, before the timing was right, before I had it all figured out.

I paid off the debt. I fixed up that house. I climbed forty feet into the air to re-roof it—despite my terror of heights—because I was more afraid of being denied a loan. Of being judged. Of going back.

And through it all, I was never once late on a bill.

Then came my bonus baby. Surprise!

Instead of crumbling, I rose again. I became a Mary Kay director in two months.

Why? Because you can't stop a woman on a mission.

Eventually, I outgrew the makeup world. I moved into real estate, then MLMs, then coaching. And just when I thought I was rebuilding a new life—my second husband died. Suddenly. No warning. Just gone.

People came to the funeral. They cried. They hugged. And then... nothing. The phone stopped ringing. The house got quiet. And I got lost.

I was heartbroken. Broke. And I had no idea who I was anymore. I remember reaching for my phone, thinking I could still call him. Grief does that. It tricks you. It freezes you.

I needed income. I needed community. But mostly, I needed purpose. So, I became an Airbnb host. It brought me people. Cash flow. A sense of usefulness. And as I healed, I got clearer.

I wanted to help women do what I had to figure out the hard way: reclaim their power. Rebuild their trust in themselves. And stop waiting for someone else to rescue them.

Because here's the truth I want to hand to you like a sacred key: You were never broken. You just forgot your own worth. And when a woman remembers her worth—everything changes.

Now, let me walk you through what this looks like in practice. The journey of becoming unsinkable isn't some vague self-help mantra. It's a daily practice. And it starts with clarity.

Clarity is Queen. Because without it, we end up treating symptoms like they're flaws. You think you have a time management issue—so you download five planners, wake up earlier, and still feel like you're failing. But the truth? It's not that you're bad with time. It's that you don't believe your needs matter enough to protect it.

The meeting you didn't want to take? You said yes because you didn't want to disappoint anyone. The hour you gave away? You didn't think your rest was worth defending. That's not poor planning. That's a worth wound.

Clarity helps you stop misdiagnosing your coping strategies as character flaws. It shows you the truth underneath the chaos. And once you *see* it—you can heal it. You stop trying to fix what was never broken and start reclaiming what was always yours.

Next? Sacred structure.

Now, I used to think "structure" was just a bossy word for boring. But sacred structure? That's freedom in disguise. It's not about rigidity. It's about rhythm. It's a daily cadence that honors *your* energy, *your* priorities, and *your* soul.

It might look like thirty minutes of quiet before your phone lights up. A journal, a cup of coffee, and three clear priorities. You protect that time like it's Beyoncé's private number. Because when your day starts with *you*, you stop living on defense. You start creating instead of reacting.

Sacred structure is a sanctuary. A cathedral of boundaries. And you are the architect.

If your "no" comes with three paragraphs of apology and a fruit basket, we need to reset your wiring. Boundaries without guilt are about recognizing that your time is valuable and your needs are valid. You don't owe anyone a novel for saying no. You don't need to backtrack or babysit someone else's disappointment.

A real boundary might sound like: "I'm not available to talk right now, but let's catch up this weekend." That's it. No guilt. No drama. Just clarity wrapped in love.

And when you start setting boundaries that way? You start creating a bubble of peace. Drama can't reach you. Guilt bounces off like a bad check. You're not being difficult. You're being deliberate. That's power.

But all of this leads to one thing: the Worthiness Reset.

Because here's what I used to believe—that worthiness was earned. That if I did nine things for other people, the tenth one would magically be my self-esteem. That was a lie.

The Worthiness Reset is the daily decision to remember: I matter because I exist. Not because I checked off thirty-seven boxes. Not because I performed. But because I breathe. Because I *am*.

You don't need to hustle for worth. You need to remember it. And when you do? Everything shifts. The people you attract. The choices you make. The voice you hear in your head when you pass a mirror.

And finally—connection over chaos.

For years, I thought being a "good communicator" meant smiling through rage and saying, "No worries!" while plotting someone's emotional demise. But real connection doesn't come from fake peace. It comes from presence.

It comes from saying, "That didn't feel respectful," instead of faking a smile and swallowing your truth. It's not about avoiding awkward. It's about choosing honesty over harmony.

When you stop performing for people who don't see you? You start attracting people who *do*. You become magnetic—not because you're perfect, but because you're real.

That's the magic. That's the freedom. That's what it means to become unsinkable.

And look, being unsinkable doesn't mean you never struggle. It means that even when life knocks the wind out of you—when grief hits, or bills pile up, or you're standing in your kitchen crying into a spoonful of peanut butter—you float anyway.

You rise anyway.

Because your self-worth has become your anchor.

You're not looking for approval. You're not auditioning for love. You're living from the truth of who you are, not the fear of who you're not.

So if you're still telling yourself, "I just need to get my act together," let me gently stop you right there.

You don't need to get your act together.

You need to get your *self* back.

Your voice. Your value. Your power. The part of you that never left— it just got buried under all the junk life threw at you.

Because when a woman knows her worth—when she walks into a room without shrinking—everything around her begins to shift. Homes change. Communities change. Economies change. The world changes.

And that starts with you.

So if you're ready to stop sinking…

If you're ready to rewrite your money story and step into a life that finally reflects your value...

Because no matter what you've been through, you can rise.

And no matter how deep the waters feel, you can become unsinkable.

Let's do this. Together.

SUE YELVINGTON

Unsinkable Sue Yelvington is a transformational coach specializing in helping women reclaim their sense of self-worth and power through the practice of radical self-love. Her journey began at just 17, when she realized that self-worth was the foundation for achieving any dream or goal. This philosophy has guided her through raising her 4 children as a single mom, and building multiple successful businesses, including Mary Kay Directorship, Real Estate, and Airbnb host. Sue helps women who have depleted themselves serving others rediscover their worth and set boundaries. Are you ready to become unsinkable?

www.SueYelvington.com

www.ingramcontent.com/pod-product-compliance
Lightning Source LLC
Chambersburg PA
CBHW061558120626
46550CB00004B/1534

* 9 7 8 1 9 5 3 5 8 6 3 5 3 *